Moving to Malta

A guide for prospective expatriates

Alex Bugeja

Table of Contents

Introduction: So, You've Lost Your Mind and Want to Move to a Rock in the Mediterranean?

Chapter 1: Malta: It's Smaller Than Your Aunt Mildred's Garden (But With More History)

Chapter 2: Visas and Permits: Prepare for Papercuts and Patience

Chapter 3: Finding a Fortress (Or Just a Flat): Maltese Real Estate Realities

Chapter 4: Banking in Malta: Where Euros Grow on Palm Trees (Not Really)

Chapter 5: Healthcare: Surprisingly Good, Once You Decipher the System

Chapter 6: Education: From Village Schools to International Baccalaureate (and Everything in Between)

Chapter 7: Working in Malta: iGaming, Finance, and Finding Your Niche (Without Falling in the Sea)

Chapter 8: The Cost of Living: Is it Cheaper Than Your Ex's Therapy Bills?

Chapter 9: Transport: Buses, Boats, and Braving the Roundabouts of Doom

Chapter 10: Maltese Culture: Embrace the Chaos (and the Pastizzi)

Chapter 11: Learning Maltese: *Mela*, You Don't *Have* To, But It Helps

Chapter 12: Food, Glorious Food: Beyond Pastizzi (But Seriously, Eat the Pastizzi)

Chapter 13: Leisure and Entertainment: Sun, Sea, and Siestas (The Holy Trinity)

Chapter 14: Making Friends: From Expats to Locals (and Avoiding the Awkward "Where Are You *Really* From?" Question)

Chapter 15: Dealing with Bureaucracy: The Maltese National Sport (After Football)

Chapter 16: Staying Safe: Crime, Cops, and Common Sense (It's Not *That* Dangerous)

Chapter 17: Pets: Bringing Your Furry (or Scaly) Friend to Paradise

Chapter 18: Utilities: Power Cuts, Water Pressure, and the Joys of Island Living

Chapter 19: Shopping: From Supermarkets to Souks (and Haggling Like a Pro)

Chapter 20: Communications: Staying Connected (Without Breaking the Bank on Roaming Charges)

Chapter 21: Driving in Malta: A Survival Guide (May Require a Therapist Afterwards)

Chapter 22: Climate: Sun, Sun, and More Sun (and the Occasional Biblical Downpour)

Chapter 23: Taxes: Don't Panic! (But Do Consult an Expert)

Chapter 24: Leaving Malta: The Reverse Culture Shock (and Missing the Pastizzi)

Chapter 25: The Final Verdict: Is Malta *Really* Worth It? (Spoiler Alert: Maybe)

Introduction: So, You've Lost Your Mind and Want to Move to a Rock in the Mediterranean?

Alright, let's not beat around the bush. You're thinking of moving to Malta. You've probably seen the Instagram photos – impossibly blue water, ancient honey-colored cities, and people seemingly living their best lives under a perpetual sun. You've maybe even read a blog post or two, whispering sweet nothings about tax benefits and a relaxed Mediterranean lifestyle. And now, here you are, contemplating a complete life upheaval. Good for you! Or, possibly, *mela* (a Maltese word you'll learn to love/hate), what have you gotten yourself into?

This book isn't going to waste your time with generic moving advice. We assume you're not a complete novice to international relocation. You know you need to pack your socks, forward your mail, and probably say goodbye to your favorite brand of instant coffee. This is Malta-specific. This is the nitty-gritty, the stuff the glossy brochures conveniently leave out. We're going to dive deep into the quirks, the challenges, and the sheer, unadulterated *strangeness* that comes with moving to a tiny island nation that's smaller than most major cities, yet somehow packs more history, bureaucracy, and passionate opinions into its borders than seems humanly possible.

Think of Malta as a delicious, multi-layered *pastizz* (another word you'll become intimately familiar with). On the surface, it's golden and inviting. But bite into it, and you'll discover a complex filling of ricotta, peas, and sometimes, a surprising kick of spice. Malta is the same. It's beautiful, yes, but it's also layered with complexities, contradictions, and a healthy dose of "what the heck just happened?" moments. This is where you realize it will be *nothing* like the brochure.

This book will be your guide through that delicious, sometimes baffling, pastizz. We'll cover everything from navigating the

Maltese visa system (prepare for an adventure) to finding a place to live that doesn't cost the equivalent of a small island nation's GDP. We'll delve into the mysteries of Maltese banking, healthcare, and education. We'll even attempt to explain the Maltese driving style, which can only be described as a thrilling (and occasionally terrifying) blend of Formula One racing and bumper cars. And you *will* need that explanation if you intend to drive in Malta - and survive the experience!

We will, of course, talk about the good stuff too. The incredible food (beyond the aforementioned pastizzi, though we'll definitely talk about those *a lot*). The vibrant culture, a fascinating blend of Mediterranean, Arabic, and British influences. The stunning beaches, the ancient ruins, the endless opportunities for exploration and adventure. Because, despite the occasional frustrations, Malta has a way of getting under your skin. It's a place that challenges you, surprises you, and ultimately, captivates you.

Why are you even *thinking* about moving halfway across the world to a place where the national language sounds like a mix of Italian, Arabic, and a cat coughing up a hairball? Maybe you're craving a slower pace of life. Maybe you're tired of the rat race and yearning for sunshine and sea. Maybe you're a digital nomad looking for a low-tax haven with good internet (well, relatively good internet… we'll get to that). Or maybe, just maybe, you're a little bit crazy. And that's perfectly okay. In fact, it's probably a prerequisite.

Because moving to Malta is not for the faint of heart. It requires a certain level of adaptability, a sense of humor, and a willingness to embrace the unexpected. If you're looking for a perfectly organized, predictable, and utterly boring existence, then, frankly, you're in the wrong place. Malta is chaotic, vibrant, and occasionally infuriating. It's a place where things rarely go according to plan, where the bureaucracy can make your head spin, and where the line between "charmingly quirky" and "utterly insane" is often blurred.

But it's also a place where you can swim in crystal-clear waters, explore ancient temples, feast on delicious food, and forge genuine connections with people from all walks of life. It's a place where you can reinvent yourself, challenge your assumptions, and discover a whole new way of living. It's a place that, despite its flaws, can steal your heart and make you never want to leave. Or, at the very least, make you appreciate a good pastizz.

So, are you ready to take the plunge? Are you prepared to embrace the chaos, navigate the bureaucracy, and learn to love (or at least tolerate) the Maltese way of life? If so, then buckle up, because you're in for a wild ride. This book is your roadmap, your survival guide, and your occasionally sarcastic companion on this journey. We'll give you the honest truth, the unvarnished reality, and the tools you need to not just survive, but thrive, in this wonderfully weird and utterly unique corner of the Mediterranean.

Don't expect us to sugarcoat anything. We're not here to sell you a dream; we're here to prepare you for reality. We'll tell you about the frustrations, the challenges, and the things that will make you want to pull your hair out. But we'll also tell you about the joys, the rewards, and the moments that will make you realize you made the right decision. Or, at the very least, a *very* interesting one.

Consider this your initiation into the expat life in Malta. It's a club with a membership fee of patience, a dress code of adaptability, and a secret handshake that involves correctly pronouncing the word "*għajn*" (good luck with that). But once you're in, you're in. You'll become part of a community of like-minded individuals who have all, in their own way, lost their minds and decided to move to a rock in the Mediterranean.

And, who knows, you might just find that it's the best decision you ever made. Or, you might end up writing your own book about the experience, warning others to stay far, far away. Either way, it's going to be an adventure. And that's half the fun, isn't it? So, grab a *Kinnie* (a Maltese soft drink you'll either love or hate), settle in, and let's get started. Your Maltese adventure awaits!

One final thing. This is probably a good time to address a question that you'll be asked *countless* times once you reach Malta: "So... why Malta?". It's up to you how you answer this question. You may have various reasons, and no doubt you will have rehearsed some of them to yourself in advance. But take it from us... there is no right answer. So relax, and embrace the madness. You have a whole new life to live and the contents of this book will help you adjust and do so to the max.

CHAPTER ONE: Malta: It's Smaller Than Your Aunt Mildred's Garden (But With More History)

Right, let's get one thing straight: Malta is *small*. We're not talking "quaint village" small. We're talking "you could probably walk across it in a day if you were really determined, extremely fit, and didn't get distracted by all the historical sites and stunning views" small. Seriously, the entire country is about 316 square kilometers (122 square miles). To put that into perspective, it's roughly the size of Denver, Colorado, or about a third of the size of New York City. Or half that of Greater London. Or around a tenth of Rhode Island, the smallest US state.

So, if you're picturing sprawling landscapes and endless horizons, adjust your expectations. You're going to become intimately familiar with every nook and cranny of this island nation. This is a place where you'll run into the same people at the grocery store, the beach, and that random festa in a village you've never heard of. This is no bad thing however and it is not hard to become part of the friendly and inclusive local community.

But don't let the size fool you. Malta packs a serious punch when it comes to history, culture, and sheer geographical diversity. It's like a miniature, Mediterranean version of a "Greatest Hits of Civilization" album. You've got Neolithic temples older than the pyramids, Roman ruins, medieval cities, Baroque churches, and remnants of British colonial rule, all crammed into an area smaller than your average national park. You will, in other words, have plenty to do.

The Maltese archipelago actually consists of three main islands: Malta (the largest), Gozo (the quieter, more rural sister island), and Comino (a tiny, mostly uninhabited island famous for its Blue Lagoon). There are also a few even smaller, uninhabited islets. Think of it as a family: Malta is the bustling, slightly stressed-out parent, Gozo is the relaxed, artistic sibling, and Comino is the wild child who just wants to swim all day.

Malta's strategic location in the middle of the Mediterranean Sea has made it a coveted prize for pretty much every major power throughout history. Phoenicians, Carthaginians, Romans, Arabs, Normans, Sicilians, the Knights of St. John, the French, and the British have all, at some point, planted their flag on Maltese soil. Each has left its mark, contributing to the unique cultural cocktail that is modern Malta. That's a long history in which each successive group has left their influence.

This means that you'll find yourself walking through ancient cities that feel like a blend of North African, Italian, and British influences. You'll hear a language that sounds like a linguistic puzzle, with roots in Arabic, Italian, and English. And you'll encounter a culture that is fiercely proud of its heritage, yet surprisingly open to new influences. So, while Malta might be small in size, it's definitely big on character. And you'll learn to appreciate that.

One of the first things you'll notice about Malta is the landscape. It's... rocky. Seriously, *very* rocky. Forget rolling green hills and lush forests. Malta is all limestone cliffs, terraced fields, and scrubby vegetation. The dominant color is a warm, honey-gold, thanks to the local Globigerina Limestone, which is used in almost all the buildings. This stone gives Maltese architecture a unique, timeless quality, and it's particularly stunning when bathed in the golden light of sunset.

The coastline is dramatic, with sheer cliffs plunging into the turquoise sea. There are hidden coves, sandy beaches (though not as many as you might think), and natural harbors that have sheltered ships for centuries. The sea is a constant presence in Maltese life, and you'll quickly learn to appreciate its beauty and its power. Be warned, however: the Maltese sun is strong. Like, *really* strong. Sunscreen is not optional; it's a survival tool.

The interior of the island is a mix of terraced fields, small villages, and ancient cities. The fields are often separated by dry-stone walls, creating a patchwork effect that's quite picturesque. The villages are typically clustered around a Baroque church, often with a central square where locals gather to socialize. And the cities, particularly Valletta (the capital) and Mdina (the former capital), are stunning examples of fortified architecture. It's worth noting that some of these have been filmed for some blockbuster productions.

Valletta, a UNESCO World Heritage site, is a masterpiece of Baroque planning. It was built by the Knights of St. John in the 16th century and is a grid of narrow streets, grand palaces, and impressive fortifications. It's a city that feels both ancient and vibrant, with a thriving cultural scene and a growing number of trendy cafes and restaurants. It's also surprisingly compact, making it easy to explore on foot. This historic and well-appointed place is a great place to spend time in.

Mdina, also known as the "Silent City," is a medieval walled city perched on a hilltop. It's a place of narrow, winding streets, imposing palaces, and breathtaking views. Stepping into Mdina is like stepping back in time, and it's easy to imagine knights in shining armor clanking down the cobblestone streets. Today, it's a popular tourist destination, but it still retains a sense of tranquility and timelessness. Be sure to visit on your first few days in Malta.

Gozo, Malta's sister island, is a different world altogether. It's smaller, quieter, and more rural than Malta, with a slower pace of life and a more laid-back atmosphere. The landscape is similar, with rocky hills and terraced fields, but it feels more untouched and less developed. Gozo is known for its stunning natural beauty, including the dramatic cliffs of Dwejra, the red sands of Ramla Bay, and the picturesque fishing village of Xlendi.

Comino, the smallest of the three main islands, is famous for its Blue Lagoon, a sheltered bay with crystal-clear turquoise waters. It's a popular spot for swimming, snorkeling, and diving, and it's a true paradise for those seeking a bit of tranquility. There's only one hotel on the island, and the permanent population is tiny, making it feel like a true escape from the hustle and bustle of modern life. You will want to visit often.

Despite its small size, Malta has a surprisingly diverse range of habitats. You'll find coastal wetlands, rocky garrigue (a type of scrubland), and even some small patches of woodland. The island is also home to a variety of wildlife, including birds, reptiles, and insects. While you're unlikely to encounter any large mammals, you might spot a Maltese wall lizard, a hedgehog, or a variety of colorful butterflies. There's more than meets the eye, here.

The climate, as mentioned earlier, is Mediterranean, with hot, dry summers and mild, wet winters. The average temperature in summer is around 30°C (86°F), but it can often feel much hotter due to the humidity. The sun is intense, and it's important to take precautions against sunburn and heatstroke. Winters are generally mild, with temperatures averaging around 15°C (59°F), but it can get surprisingly chilly, especially when the wind picks up.

Rainfall is concentrated in the winter months, and it can be quite heavy at times. Malta is prone to occasional storms, which can bring strong winds and torrential rain. These storms can be quite dramatic, but they usually pass quickly, leaving behind clear skies and fresh air. Be sure to take appropriate care at such times, especially if you are near to the coast in an exposed area. However these storms are not that common.

The Maltese people are known for their warmth, hospitality, and strong sense of community. They are fiercely proud of their heritage and their unique culture. Family is incredibly important in Maltese society, and you'll often see multiple generations living together or gathering for large family meals. Religion also plays a significant role in Maltese life, with the vast majority of the population identifying as Roman Catholic. And you'll soon realize the important this has.

The Maltese are also known for their love of festas, religious celebrations held in honor of a village's patron saint. These festas are colorful, vibrant affairs, with fireworks, processions, band marches, and plenty of food and drink. They're a great way to experience Maltese culture and to witness the strong sense of community that exists in the villages. So be prepared for a noisy and lively atmosphere - and a late night.

The official languages of Malta are Maltese and English. Maltese is a Semitic language with roots in Arabic, Italian, and English. It's a unique and fascinating language, and it's the only Semitic language written in the Latin alphabet. English is widely spoken, especially in the tourist areas and in business, so you shouldn't have any trouble communicating. However, learning a few basic Maltese phrases will be appreciated by the locals.

The Maltese are generally quite tolerant and welcoming of foreigners, but it's important to be respectful of their culture and traditions. Dress modestly when visiting churches, and be mindful of noise levels, especially in residential areas. The Maltese are also quite direct in their communication style, which can sometimes be misinterpreted as rudeness by those from more reserved cultures. Be sure to bear all of this in mind.

One of the things that surprises many newcomers to Malta is the sheer number of public holidays. There are 14 public holidays in total, which is significantly more than in many other European countries. This is partly due to the strong religious influence in Maltese society, with many of the holidays being religious feast days. It also reflects the Maltese love of a good celebration. It's something you may as well get used to.

Another quirk of Maltese life is the siesta, a traditional afternoon break taken during the hottest part of the day. While the siesta is becoming less common in the larger towns and cities, it's still widely observed in the villages. Many shops and businesses close for a few hours in the afternoon, reopening in the late afternoon or early evening. So don't be surprised if you arrive somewhere and it is closed.

So, there you have it: a brief overview of Malta, the tiny island nation that's big on history, culture, and surprises. It's a place that will challenge your preconceptions, broaden your horizons, and probably leave you with a permanent tan. It's not perfect, but it's certainly never boring. And, as you'll soon discover, it has a way of getting under your skin and making you feel like you belong. Even if you're still not quite sure how to pronounce "*għajn*".

CHAPTER TWO: Visas and Permits: Prepare for Papercuts and Patience

Okay, deep breaths. We're about to tackle the beast that is Maltese bureaucracy. Specifically, the visa and permit system. If you're from an EU/EEA country, you can skip ahead, smugly sipping your *Kinnie* and enjoying your freedom of movement. This chapter is for the rest of us, the mere mortals who require official stamps, endless forms, and the patience of a saint to legally reside on this sun-drenched rock. This might be your first experience of the Maltese way of doing things.

First, let's clarify the difference between a visa and a permit. Think of a visa as your "permission to enter" ticket. It's typically a sticker in your passport that allows you to stay in Malta for a specific period, usually up to 90 days. A permit, on the other hand, is your "permission to stay" card. It's what you need if you plan to live, work, or study in Malta for a longer period. Get this straight.

Now, the type of visa or permit you need depends on your nationality, your reason for moving to Malta, and your tolerance for paperwork. Malta, like any country, has a variety of options, each with its own set of requirements, processing times, and associated headaches. The good news is that the information is (mostly) available online. The bad news is that navigating the official websites can feel like exploring a labyrinth designed by a sadist with a fondness for acronyms.

The main authority you'll be dealing with is Identity Malta, the government agency responsible for, well, pretty much everything related to identity, citizenship, and residency. Their website is your starting point, but be warned: it's a dense jungle of information. You'll encounter terms like "Single Permit," "Key Employee Initiative," "Nomad Residence Permit," and a whole host of other phrases that sound like they were invented by a committee of bureaucrats trying to justify their existence.

Let's break down some of the most common visa/permit options for prospective expats. Remember, this is not exhaustive, and the rules can change, so always double-check the latest information on the Identity Malta website or consult with an immigration lawyer (highly recommended, if you can afford it). This is important because it will affect your chances of success. And we don't want you to be embarking on a wild goose chase.

If you're a non-EU/EEA citizen planning to work in Malta, you'll likely need a Single Permit. This combines both a work permit and a residence permit into one application. It's the most common route for employed expats, but it's also one of the more complex processes. Your prospective employer typically initiates the application, and you'll need to provide a mountain of documents, including your employment contract, proof of qualifications, a clean criminal record, and evidence that you have a place to live.

The Key Employee Initiative (KEI) is a fast-tracked version of the Single Permit for highly skilled workers in specific sectors. If you qualify, it can significantly speed up the process, but the criteria are strict. You'll need to earn a minimum salary, have relevant qualifications and experience, and your employer will need to demonstrate that they couldn't find a suitable candidate within the EU/EEA. It is definitely worth looking into if any of the foregoing apply to you.

The Nomad Residence Permit is a relatively new option aimed at digital nomads and remote workers. It allows you to live in Malta while working for a foreign company or as a freelancer. You'll need to prove that you earn a minimum monthly income, have health insurance, and, crucially, that your work can be done remotely. This has become a popular option in recent years, reflecting the changing nature of work. This is a great option.

If you're planning to study in Malta, you'll need a student visa/permit. The requirements vary depending on the length and type of your course, but generally, you'll need to provide proof of acceptance from a recognized educational institution, evidence of sufficient funds to support yourself, and health insurance. You'll also need to demonstrate that you have a genuine intention to study and that you plan to leave Malta after completing your course. This is relatively common.

For those with deep pockets, there's the Malta Permanent Residence Programme (MPRP). This is essentially a "golden visa" scheme that grants permanent residency in exchange for a significant investment in Malta. It's not cheap – we're talking hundreds of thousands of euros in property purchases, government contributions, and mandatory donations – but it offers a fast track to residency and, eventually, potential citizenship. Consider it if you have the means.

There's also a retirement visa/permit option for those who want to spend their golden years soaking up the Maltese sun. You'll need to prove that you have sufficient financial resources to support yourself without working, have health insurance, and a clean criminal record. It's a relatively straightforward process, but it doesn't grant you the right to work in Malta. So you should be sure that it is suitable.

Regardless of the specific visa/permit you're applying for, there are some common threads. You'll need patience, persistence, and a high tolerance for bureaucracy. The process can be slow, frustrating, and seemingly illogical at times. Be prepared for long waiting times, requests for additional documents, and the occasional communication breakdown. It's all part of the Maltese experience. And it's all part of the "fun".

It's highly recommended to gather all your required documents *before* you start the application process. This will save you time and frustration later on. Make copies of everything, and keep the originals in a safe place. You'll likely need to provide certified translations of any documents that aren't in English or Maltese. This can add to the cost and complexity, so factor that in. But it is absolutely essential.

Once you've submitted your application, be prepared to wait. Processing times can vary significantly depending on the type of permit, the time of year, and the workload of the Identity Malta staff. It's not uncommon for applications to take several months, or even longer, to be processed. You can check the status of your application online, but don't expect frequent updates. It's a waiting game, like so many Maltese things.

While you're waiting, it's a good idea to familiarize yourself with Maltese laws and regulations. You're expected to abide by the same rules as Maltese citizens, and ignorance of the law is not an excuse. Pay particular attention to traffic laws (we'll cover those in more detail later), noise regulations, and any rules related to your specific visa/permit. Maltese culture can be unforgiving of infringements of the law.

Once your application is approved, you'll receive your residence permit, which is typically a card with your photo, personal details, and the type of permit you've been granted. This card is your official identification in Malta, and you should carry it with you at all times. You'll need it to open a bank account, rent a property, access healthcare, and generally prove that you're legally allowed to be in the country.

Renewing your permit is usually a less painful process than the initial application, but it still requires some effort. You'll need to submit a renewal application before your current permit expires, and you'll need to provide updated documents, such as proof of continued employment or financial stability. It's a good idea to start the renewal process well in advance of the expiry date, just in case there are any delays.

One common complaint among expats is the inconsistency of the application process. Different case officers might interpret the rules differently, and what worked for one person might not work for another. It can be frustrating, but it's important to remain polite and respectful, even when you feel like tearing your hair out. Losing your temper with Identity Malta staff is unlikely to speed up your application.

Another tip: don't be afraid to ask for help. There are numerous online forums and Facebook groups dedicated to expats in Malta, and they can be a valuable source of information and support. You can ask questions, share experiences, and get advice from people who have been through the same process. Just be aware that online advice is not always accurate, so double-check everything with official sources.

If you're feeling overwhelmed by the paperwork and the bureaucracy, consider hiring an immigration lawyer or consultant. They can guide you through the process, ensure that your application is complete and accurate, and liaise with Identity Malta on your behalf. It's an additional expense, but it can save you a lot of time, stress, and potential mistakes. It is often, in fact, well worth the investment.

Finally, remember that the visa/permit process is just the first hurdle. Once you've successfully navigated that, you'll have a whole new set of challenges to face, from finding a place to live to understanding the Maltese driving style. But don't worry, we'll cover all of that in the following chapters. For now, focus on getting your paperwork in order, practicing your patience, and maybe investing in a good stress ball.

The Maltese visa and permit system is, frankly, a bit of a mess. It's overly complicated, often inconsistent, and can be incredibly frustrating to navigate. But it's also a necessary evil if you want to live and work in Malta legally. So, embrace the challenge, prepare for the papercuts, and remember that the reward – a life in the Mediterranean sun – is (hopefully) worth the effort. Just don't expect it to be easy.

And one final, crucial piece of advice: never, *ever* overstay your visa or permit. The consequences can be severe, including fines, deportation, and a ban from re-entering Malta. It's simply not worth the risk. Play by the rules, even if the rules seem arbitrary and illogical. It's the Maltese way. And, as you'll soon learn, adapting to the Maltese way is the key to surviving, and even thriving, on this quirky little island. Good luck and it's all worth it in the end.

CHAPTER THREE: Finding a Fortress (Or Just a Flat): Maltese Real Estate Realities

Right, you've conquered the visa beast (or at least survived the first round). Now, you need a place to live. Unless you're planning on sleeping on one of Malta's admittedly beautiful beaches (not recommended – the sand gets *everywhere*), you're going to have to navigate the Maltese real estate market. And, *mela*, it's an experience. It's a market unlike any other, and is quirky, to say the least.

Think of the Maltese property market as a game of Monopoly, but with more shouting, more hand gestures, and a significantly higher chance of ending up with a property that's older than your great-great-grandmother. You'll encounter everything from centuries-old palazzos with secret gardens to modern apartment blocks with questionable plumbing. You'll deal with estate agents who range from charmingly helpful to… well, let's just say "less so." And you'll learn to decipher property descriptions that would make a seasoned poet blush with their creative use of language.

First, let's dispel a myth: Malta is *not* a cheap place to live, especially when it comes to housing. While the cost of living overall might be lower than in some other European countries, property prices, particularly in popular areas, have skyrocketed in recent years. This is due to a combination of factors, including increased foreign investment, a booming economy (pre-COVID, anyway), and, you know, the fact that it's a tiny island with limited space.

So, unless you're a millionaire with a penchant for crumbling farmhouses, be prepared to adjust your expectations. That dream of a sprawling villa with a sea view and a swimming pool? It might exist, but it'll cost you a small fortune. A more realistic option for most expats is an apartment, either in a modern block or a converted townhouse. Houses of character, with original features, are also popular, but they tend to be more expensive and often require significant renovation work.

The most popular areas for expats are generally concentrated around the central and northern parts of Malta. Sliema and St. Julian's are the hotspots, known for their lively atmosphere, seafront promenades, and abundance of shops, restaurants, and bars. They're also close to many of the iGaming and finance companies that employ a large number of expats. However, they're also the most expensive areas, and parking can be a nightmare.

Valletta, the capital, is another popular choice, offering a more historical and cultural setting. It's becoming increasingly gentrified, with a growing number of trendy apartments and boutique hotels. However, it's still relatively quiet in the evenings, and it can be difficult to find parking. Gzira and Msida, located near the University of Malta, are more affordable options, popular with students and young professionals. They're well-connected by public transport, but they can be quite noisy and congested.

Further north, you'll find towns like Mellieha, Bugibba, and Qawra, which are popular with tourists and offer a more relaxed pace of life. They're generally more affordable than Sliema and St. Julian's, but they're also further away from the main business hubs. Gozo, Malta's sister island, is another option for those seeking a quieter, more rural lifestyle. Property prices are generally lower on Gozo, but you'll need to factor in the ferry commute to Malta if you plan to work there.

Once you've decided on a general area, it's time to start your property search. There are several ways to go about this. You can use online property portals, contact estate agents directly, or simply wander around the streets looking for "For Rent" or "For Sale" signs. The latter option can be surprisingly effective, as some landlords prefer to advertise locally rather than online. It's also a good way to get a feel for the different neighborhoods.

The main online property portals in Malta are similar to those you'll find in other countries. They allow you to search for properties based on location, price, size, and other criteria. However, be aware that the photos and descriptions can sometimes be misleading. A "sea view" might mean a glimpse of the Mediterranean from a tiny balcony, and a "spacious" apartment might be anything but. It's always best to view a property in person before making any commitments.

Estate agents are a common feature of the Maltese property market, and they can be a useful resource, especially if you're new to the island. They can help you find properties that match your requirements, arrange viewings, and negotiate with landlords or sellers. However, it's important to choose your agent carefully. Some agents are more reputable and professional than others, and it's not uncommon to hear stories of expats being overcharged or misled.

When dealing with estate agents, be clear about your budget and your requirements. Don't be afraid to ask questions, and don't feel pressured to make a decision quickly. It's also a good idea to get recommendations from other expats or to check online reviews before choosing an agent. Remember that the agent is working for the landlord or seller, not for you, so their primary interest is in closing a deal, not necessarily in finding you the perfect property.

When viewing properties, pay close attention to the details. Check the water pressure, the condition of the appliances, and the general state of repair. Ask about the age of the building, the type of construction, and any known issues. Don't be afraid to open cupboards, flush toilets, and turn on taps. It's better to be thorough and identify any potential problems before you sign a contract. It will save you headaches in the long run.

If you're renting, be sure to read the contract carefully before signing. Pay particular attention to the terms of the lease, the deposit amount, and any clauses related to maintenance and repairs. Maltese rental contracts are typically for one year, but shorter or longer leases are sometimes possible. The deposit is usually equivalent to one or two months' rent, and it should be returned to you at the end of the lease, provided you haven't damaged the property.

It's also important to clarify who is responsible for paying the utility bills (water, electricity, and internet). In some cases, the bills are included in the rent, but more often, they're the tenant's responsibility. Be aware that utility costs in Malta can be quite high, especially in the summer when air conditioning is essential. Ask the landlord or agent for an estimate of the average monthly bills to get an idea of what to expect.

If you're buying a property, the process is more complex and involves a number of legal and financial steps. You'll need to engage a notary, who will act as a neutral intermediary between you and the seller. The notary will conduct searches on the property, draw up the preliminary agreement (known as the "konvenju"), and eventually, the final deed of sale. It's also advisable to hire a lawyer to represent your interests and to ensure that everything is done correctly.

The "konvenju" is a legally binding agreement that sets out the terms of the sale, including the price, the deposit, and the completion date. Once the "konvenju" is signed, you'll typically pay a deposit of 10% of the purchase price. The remaining balance is paid upon signing the final deed, usually within three months. During this period, the notary will conduct searches to ensure that the property is free of any encumbrances, such as mortgages or debts.

Be aware that there are additional costs associated with buying property in Malta, including notary fees, stamp duty, and registration fees. These costs can add up to a significant amount, so it's important to factor them into your budget. It's also advisable to get a survey of the property before committing to the purchase, especially if it's an older building. This will identify any structural issues or hidden problems that could cost you money in the long run.

One quirk of the Maltese property market is the prevalence of "ground rent." This is a form of land ownership where you own the building, but not the land it sits on. The land is owned by a third party, usually the Church or the government, and you pay an annual ground rent fee. Ground rent can be either temporary (expiring after a certain number of years) or perpetual (lasting forever). It's important to understand the terms of the ground rent before buying a property, as it can affect its value and your ability to sell it in the future.

Another thing to be aware of is the issue of unfinished properties. It's not uncommon to see buildings that are partially constructed or left in a state of disrepair. This can be due to a variety of reasons, including financial difficulties, planning disputes, or simply the Maltese tendency to take things slowly. While unfinished properties might be cheaper, they can also be a risky investment, as there's no guarantee that they'll ever be completed.

Finding a place to live in Malta can be a challenging, but ultimately rewarding, experience. It requires patience, persistence, and a good sense of humor. You'll encounter quirky landlords, confusing contracts, and properties that defy description. But you'll also find stunning views, charming neighborhoods, and a sense of community that's hard to find elsewhere. And, if you're lucky, you might even find a fortress to call your own. Or, at the very least, a flat with decent plumbing.

CHAPTER FOUR: Banking in Malta: Where Euros Grow on Palm Trees (Not Really)

Alright, you've secured your visa (somehow), found a place to live (that hopefully has running water), and now it's time to tackle the thrilling world of Maltese banking. Now, before you conjure images of palm trees laden with euro notes, let's get one thing straight: money doesn't *actually* grow on trees here. Though, given the Maltese penchant for creative accounting, you might occasionally wonder. This may be the case when you encounter some of the hidden charges.

Opening a bank account in Malta is, like most things on this island, an experience. It's a blend of modern convenience and old-fashioned bureaucracy, with a dash of "what just happened?" thrown in for good measure. Think of it as a financial obstacle course, where the obstacles are forms, the hurdles are unexpected fees, and the finish line is a functional bank account that doesn't make you want to tear your hair out. You might encounter the latter.

First, let's talk about the banks themselves. Malta has a mix of local and international banks. The major players are Bank of Valletta (BOV), HSBC Malta, and APS Bank. There are also a few smaller banks, such as BNF Bank and Lombard Bank, as well as some international banks with a limited presence. Each bank has its own pros and cons, and the best choice for you will depend on your individual needs and preferences.

Bank of Valletta (BOV) is the largest bank in Malta, with a wide network of branches and ATMs. It's a bit like the grand old dame of Maltese banking – established, reliable, but perhaps a little set in her ways. HSBC Malta, part of the global HSBC group, offers a more international perspective and a wider range of services. It's generally considered to be more technologically advanced than BOV, but it also tends to be more expensive.

APS Bank is a smaller, community-focused bank that prides itself on its ethical and sustainable approach. It's a good option if you're looking for a bank with a strong social conscience, but its branch network is more limited than BOV or HSBC. BNF Bank and Lombard Bank are also smaller players, offering a range of personal and business banking services. They tend to be more flexible and customer-focused than the larger banks, but their services might be more limited.

Choosing a bank is the first hurdle. The next step is actually opening an account. And this, my friend, is where the fun (or, more accurately, the mild frustration) begins. Be prepared for paperwork. Lots and lots of paperwork. You'll need your passport, your residence permit (once you have it), proof of address (a utility bill or rental contract), and a reference letter from your previous bank. You might also be asked to provide proof of income, employment details, and a detailed explanation of your financial history.

The process can vary depending on the bank and the type of account you're opening, but generally, it involves filling out numerous forms, providing copies of your documents, and attending an in-person interview at a branch. The interview is usually a formality, but it can be a bit daunting, especially if you're not fluent in Maltese or English. The bank staff will ask you about your reasons for opening an account, your expected transactions, and your financial background.

It's important to be honest and upfront with the bank. Maltese banks are subject to strict anti-money laundering regulations, and they take their compliance obligations very seriously. Any hint of suspicious activity or incomplete information can lead to delays or even the rejection of your application. So, be prepared to answer questions about your source of funds, your employment history, and your overall financial situation. It's not personal; it's just the way things are done here.

Once your application is approved, you'll be issued with a bank account number, a debit card (usually a Visa or Mastercard), and access to online banking. The debit card can be used for ATM withdrawals, point-of-sale purchases, and online transactions. Online banking allows you to manage your account, transfer funds, pay bills, and generally keep track of your finances. However, be aware that the online banking platforms of some Maltese banks can be a bit... clunky.

Maltese banks offer a range of accounts, including current accounts, savings accounts, and term deposit accounts. Current accounts are designed for everyday transactions, while savings accounts offer a higher interest rate but may have restrictions on withdrawals. Term deposit accounts offer the highest interest rates, but your money is locked in for a fixed period. The interest rates on Maltese bank accounts are generally quite low, reflecting the current economic climate.

One thing to be aware of is the fees. Maltese banks are notorious for their fees, which can range from the understandable (ATM withdrawal fees) to the downright baffling (monthly account maintenance fees, fees for receiving bank statements, fees for... well, just about anything). It's important to read the fine print carefully and understand the fee structure of your chosen bank before opening an account. Otherwise, you might be in for some unpleasant surprises.

Another quirk of Maltese banking is the chequebook. Yes, chequebooks still exist in Malta, and they're still used surprisingly frequently. You might need to write a cheque to pay your rent, your utility bills, or even your groceries. It's a bit of a throwback to a bygone era, but it's just one of those things you have to get used to in Malta. Just be sure to keep your chequebook in a safe place, as cheque fraud is not unheard of.

Transferring money to and from Malta can also be a bit of a challenge. While SEPA (Single Euro Payments Area) transfers within the EU are generally straightforward and inexpensive, transfers to or from countries outside the SEPA zone can be more complicated and costly. You might encounter delays, high fees, and unfavorable exchange rates. It's a good idea to research the best options for international money transfers before you move to Malta.

One popular option for international money transfers is to use a specialist provider, such as Wise (formerly TransferWise) or Revolut. These companies typically offer better exchange rates and lower fees than traditional banks. They're also generally faster and more convenient, with online platforms and mobile apps that make it easy to send and receive money. However, it's important to compare the different providers and their fees to find the best option for your specific needs.

Another thing to consider is your credit rating. If you plan to apply for a loan or a credit card in Malta, your credit history will be taken into account. Unfortunately, your credit rating from your home country might not be recognized in Malta. This means you might have to start building your credit history from scratch. This can be a slow and frustrating process, but it's important to be patient and persistent.

One way to build your credit history in Malta is to open a local bank account and use it responsibly. Pay your bills on time, avoid going overdrawn, and generally demonstrate that you're a reliable borrower. You can also apply for a secured credit card, which is a credit card that's backed by a cash deposit. This can be a good way to build your credit rating without taking on too much risk.

Once you have a Maltese bank account, you'll need to register with the Inland Revenue Department (IRD) and obtain a tax identification number (TIN). This is required for all residents of Malta, regardless of whether you're employed, self-employed, or retired. The TIN is used for all tax-related matters, including filing your annual tax return and paying any taxes you owe. The process of obtaining a TIN is relatively straightforward, but it requires another visit to a government office and, of course, more paperwork.

Speaking of taxes, it's important to understand the Maltese tax system. Malta has a relatively low tax rate compared to some other

European countries, but it's still important to be aware of your tax obligations. If you're employed, your employer will deduct tax from your salary each month under the Final Settlement System (FSS). If you're self-employed, you'll need to file an annual tax return and pay your taxes directly to the IRD.

Malta also has a number of tax incentives for expats, particularly those working in certain sectors or investing in the country. These incentives can significantly reduce your tax burden, but it's important to seek professional advice to ensure that you're complying with all the rules and regulations. There are numerous tax advisors and accountants in Malta who specialize in expat tax matters.

Banking in Malta is not always a smooth or straightforward process. It can be frustrating, time-consuming, and occasionally baffling. But it's also a necessary part of life on this island. So, embrace the challenge, learn to navigate the bureaucracy, and don't be afraid to ask for help. And, most importantly, remember that even if money doesn't grow on trees in Malta, the sunshine, the sea, and the *pastizzi* are (almost) free.

And now for a few practical tips to help you on your banking journey in Malta. Do shop around and compare the different banks before making a decision. Don't be afraid to ask questions and clarify anything you don't understand. Make sure that you get a list of all charges in writing - and make sure you go through them. Don't assume anything.

Be prepared for paperwork and long waiting times. Gather all your required documents before you start the application process. Be honest and upfront with the bank about your financial situation. Read the fine print carefully and understand the fee structure of your chosen bank. Consider using a specialist provider for international money transfers. Build your credit history in Malta by using your bank account responsibly.

Register with the Inland Revenue Department and obtain a tax identification number. Familiarize yourself with the Maltese tax system and seek professional advice if needed. And don't despair. The banking system *will* frustrate you at some point. But be patient!

Banking in Malta might not be the most glamorous aspect of expat life, but it's an essential one. With a little patience, persistence, and a good dose of humor, you'll navigate the system and (eventually) get your finances in order. And then you can finally relax, enjoy the sunshine, and maybe even treat yourself to a *pastizz* (or two). You'll have earned it. After all, you've just conquered Maltese banking.

CHAPTER FIVE: Healthcare: Surprisingly Good, Once You Decipher the System

Right, let's talk about something that might give you a slight anxiety attack, especially if you're coming from a country with a, shall we say, *less-than-stellar* healthcare system: getting sick in Malta. Don't panic. Despite its size, Malta boasts a surprisingly robust healthcare system, ranked consistently high in international comparisons. It's a mix of public and private options, offering a good standard of care, once you figure out how it all works. Which, naturally, is the tricky part.

Think of the Maltese healthcare system as a two-headed beast. One head is the public system, funded by national insurance contributions and providing free (or very low-cost) healthcare to all legal residents. The other head is the private system, offering faster access and more luxurious facilities, but at a price. Choosing between the two, or opting for a combination of both, is a personal decision based on your budget, your health needs, and your tolerance for waiting rooms.

The cornerstone of the public system is Mater Dei Hospital, a large, modern hospital located in Msida, near the University of Malta. It's the main general hospital for the entire country, offering a wide range of services, from emergency care to specialized surgery. It's generally well-equipped and staffed by qualified doctors and nurses, but it can get very busy, especially during peak hours. Waiting times for non-emergency appointments and procedures can be lengthy. This is, however, not unusual in public healthcare systems.

In addition to Mater Dei, there are a number of health centers and clinics scattered throughout Malta and Gozo. These provide primary care services, such as GP consultations, vaccinations, and basic diagnostic tests. They're generally more accessible than Mater Dei, with shorter waiting times, but they offer a more limited range of services. If you need to see a specialist, you'll typically need a referral from a GP at a health center. It is a hub and spoke system.

To access the public healthcare system, you'll need to be registered as a legal resident and have a social security number. Once you're registered, you'll be assigned a GP at your local health center. You can then make appointments to see your GP for routine check-ups, minor illnesses, and referrals to specialists. Emergency care is always free at Mater Dei, regardless of your residency status. But again, for any emergencies you should be ready for a long wait.

One of the perks of the public system is that prescription medications are heavily subsidized. If you have a chronic condition that requires regular medication, you can apply for a "Schedule V" card, which entitles you to free medication. The process of obtaining a Schedule V card can be a bit bureaucratic, but it's worth it if you're on long-term medication. And this represents a huge cost saving. So it is worth going through the bureaucracy.

The private healthcare system in Malta offers a faster, more personalized alternative to the public system. There are several private hospitals and clinics, offering a wide range of services, from GP consultations to cosmetic surgery. The quality of care is generally excellent, and the facilities are often more modern and comfortable than in the public system. However, private healthcare comes at a cost. You'll need to pay for consultations, treatments, and medications out of pocket, or through private health insurance.

Private health insurance is a popular option for expats in Malta, as it provides access to private healthcare without the hefty price tag. There are several insurance providers offering a range of plans, from basic coverage to comprehensive policies that cover everything from GP visits to dental care. The cost of private health insurance varies depending on your age, your health status, and the level of coverage you choose. It's important to compare the different plans and choose one that meets your individual needs and budget.

One of the advantages of private healthcare is the shorter waiting times. You can typically get an appointment with a GP or a specialist within a few days, or even on the same day. This can be a major benefit if you have a non-emergency condition that requires prompt attention. Private hospitals also tend to offer more comfortable facilities, such as private rooms and en-suite bathrooms. However, it's important to remember that private healthcare is not necessarily *better* than public healthcare, just faster and more convenient.

Many expats opt for a combination of public and private healthcare. They might use the public system for routine check-ups and minor illnesses, and rely on private insurance for more serious conditions or emergencies. This allows them to benefit from the free or low-cost services of the public system while still having access to the faster and more personalized care of the private system. It's a pragmatic approach that balances cost and convenience.

One thing to be aware of is that some doctors in Malta work in both the public and private systems. This means you might see the same doctor at Mater Dei and at a private clinic. The difference is that in the private clinic, you'll be paying for their time, while in the public system, their services are covered by your national insurance contributions. This can sometimes lead to confusion, so it's important to clarify whether you're being seen as a public or private patient.

Another quirk of the Maltese healthcare system is the role of the pharmacist. Pharmacists in Malta are highly trained and can provide advice on a wide range of minor ailments. They can also dispense certain medications without a prescription, such as antibiotics for common infections. This can be a convenient option if you have a minor illness and don't want to wait for a GP appointment. However, it's important to remember that pharmacists are not doctors, and they should not be used as a substitute for medical advice.

If you have a pre-existing medical condition, it's important to bring all your relevant medical records with you to Malta. This will help your new doctor understand your medical history and ensure that you receive appropriate care. It's also a good idea to have a list of any medications you're taking, including the generic names and dosages. This will be helpful if you need to obtain a prescription in Malta. Translating these is not essential, but it might be.

If you're pregnant and planning to give birth in Malta, you have the option of choosing between public and private maternity care. Mater Dei Hospital has a modern maternity unit, offering a range of services, from antenatal care to postnatal support. Private hospitals also offer maternity services, often with more luxurious facilities and a more personalized approach. The choice is yours, based on your preferences and your budget.

One thing to note is that abortion is illegal in Malta, except in cases where the mother's life is at risk. This is a controversial issue, and it's important to be aware of the law if you're considering becoming pregnant while living in Malta. Contraception, on the other hand, is widely available and easily accessible. You can obtain contraception from pharmacies, health centers, and family planning clinics.

Mental health services in Malta are still developing, and access to mental healthcare can be challenging. There is a state-run mental health hospital, Mount Carmel Hospital, but it has a reputation for being outdated and understaffed. Private mental healthcare is available, but it can be expensive. There are also a number of NGOs and charities offering mental health support services, such as counseling and support groups.

If you have a mental health condition, it's important to discuss your needs with your doctor before moving to Malta. They can advise you on the best course of action and help you find appropriate support services. It's also a good idea to bring any relevant medical records with you, including information about your diagnosis and treatment. And this will help to ensure continuity of care. This will assist the professionals.

In an emergency, you should call 112, which is the European emergency number. This number can be used to contact the ambulance service, the police, or the fire department. If you need urgent medical attention, you should go to the Emergency Department at Mater Dei Hospital. Be prepared for a wait, as the Emergency Department can get very busy. Bring your ID card, your European Health Insurance Card (EHIC) if you have one, and any relevant medical information.

If you're from an EU/EEA country, you're entitled to free or reduced-cost healthcare in Malta under the EHIC scheme. The EHIC covers you for medically necessary treatment, including emergency care, GP consultations, and hospital stays. However, it doesn't cover you for non-emergency treatment or for private healthcare. It's important to have your EHIC with you when accessing healthcare in Malta. And be sure to keep it somewhere safe.

If you're from a non-EU/EEA country, you'll need to have private health insurance to cover your healthcare costs in Malta. Make sure your insurance policy covers you for all the services you might need, including emergency care, GP consultations, specialist appointments, and hospital stays. It's also a good idea to check whether your insurance provider has a direct billing agreement with any hospitals or clinics in Malta.

The Maltese healthcare system, like any system, has its pros and cons. The public system is affordable and accessible, but it can be slow and bureaucratic. The private system is faster and more convenient, but it comes at a cost. The key is to understand how the system works and to choose the options that best meet your individual needs and budget. And, as always in Malta, be prepared for a bit of a learning curve.

And now for a few practical tips. Register with a GP at your local health center as soon as possible after arriving in Malta. Get private health insurance if you're not covered by the EHIC or if you want access to private healthcare. Bring all your relevant medical records with you to Malta. Learn the emergency number

(112) and keep it in a handy place. Be prepared for waiting times, especially in the public system.

Familiarize yourself with the role of the pharmacist and don't be afraid to ask for their advice on minor ailments. If you have a chronic condition, apply for a Schedule V card to get free medication. If you're pregnant, research your options for maternity care. Be aware of the law on abortion in Malta. Seek professional help if you're struggling with your mental health. And don't worry. The Maltese healthcare system may be a little different.

Healthcare in Malta might seem a bit daunting at first, but with a little research and preparation, you'll be able to navigate the system and access the care you need. And remember, the Maltese are generally a healthy bunch, thanks to the Mediterranean diet, the sunshine, and the relaxed pace of life. So, chances are, you'll spend more time enjoying the beach than you will in a doctor's waiting room. Unless, of course, you get addicted to *pastizzi*. Then all bets are off.

CHAPTER SIX: Education: From Village Schools to International Baccalaureate (and Everything in Between)

So, you've got the housing, banking, and healthcare (mostly) sorted. Now, if you've got kids, or are planning on pursuing further education yourself, you'll need to grapple with the Maltese education system. It's another one of those delightful Maltese mixes: a blend of state-funded, church-run, and independent schools, offering everything from traditional Maltese curricula to international qualifications. Think of it as a scholastic buffet, with options to suit every taste (and budget). You *will* find something.

First, let's get the legal stuff out of the way. Education in Malta is compulsory for children between the ages of 5 and 16. This applies to all children residing in Malta, regardless of their nationality. You have a choice of sending your children to state schools (free), church schools (also free, but with some voluntary donations), or independent/international schools (fee-paying). The choice is yours, but each option has its own set of pros, cons, and, naturally, quirks.

State schools are run by the government and follow the National Curriculum Framework (NCF). They're generally well-resourced, with qualified teachers, but they can be large and sometimes overcrowded. The primary language of instruction is Maltese, although English is also taught as a core subject. This can be a challenge for expat children who don't speak Maltese, but it can also be a great opportunity for them to learn a new language and immerse themselves in the local culture.

The school year in Malta runs from September to June, with breaks for Christmas, Easter, and a long summer holiday. The school day typically starts around 8:30 am and finishes around 2:30 pm, although this can vary slightly depending on the school. Extracurricular activities, such as sports, music, and drama, are often offered after school hours, but these might be limited compared to what you're used to in other countries. There are plenty of things to do.

Church schools, as the name suggests, are run by the Catholic Church. They're funded by the government, but they also rely on voluntary donations from parents. They follow the same National Curriculum Framework as state schools, but they also have a strong religious ethos. This means that religious education is a core subject, and Catholic values are integrated into the school day. While most church schools welcome children of all faiths, it's important to be aware of the religious aspect.

Church schools are generally well-regarded in Malta, and they often have a strong sense of community. They tend to be smaller than state schools, with a more personalized approach to education. However, admission to church schools can be competitive, and there's often a waiting list. Preference is usually given to Catholic children, but non-Catholic children are also admitted if places are available. The Church aspect is something to consider. But bear in mind that the Maltese are largely Catholic.

Independent and international schools offer a more diverse range of curricula and teaching styles. They're fee-paying, and the fees can be quite high, especially for the more prestigious schools. However, they often offer smaller class sizes, better facilities, and a wider range of extracurricular activities. They also tend to have a more international student body, which can be a benefit for expat children who are looking for a more familiar environment. This might, in fact, be ideal.

The most common international curricula offered in Malta are the International Baccalaureate (IB) and the British GCSE and A-Level systems. The IB is a globally recognized qualification that's highly regarded by universities around the world. It's a rigorous program that emphasizes critical thinking, independent learning, and international-mindedness. The GCSE and A-Level systems are the standard qualifications for students in the UK, and they're also widely accepted by universities internationally. You have several choices.

There are several international schools in Malta, catering to different age groups and offering different curricula. Some of the most well-known include Verdala International School, QSI International School of Malta, and St. Edward's College (which, despite its name, is a school, not a college). These schools tend to have excellent facilities, including modern classrooms, science labs, sports fields, and libraries. They also offer a wide range of extracurricular activities, from sports and music to debating and Model United Nations.

If you're considering an international school, it's important to visit the school, meet the teachers, and get a feel for the environment. Each school has its own unique atmosphere and ethos, and it's important to find one that's a good fit for your child. You should also inquire about the school's admissions policy, its fees, and its waiting list. Some international schools have long waiting lists, especially for the more popular year groups. It will help if you plan ahead.

For younger children, there are also a number of pre-schools and kindergartens in Malta. These are not compulsory, but they're a popular option for working parents. They provide a safe and stimulating environment for young children to learn and play, and they can help prepare them for primary school. Pre-schools and kindergartens can be state-run, church-run, or independent, and the fees vary accordingly. But they are certainly worth considering.

If you're planning to pursue higher education in Malta, you have several options. The main institution is the University of Malta, a public university that offers a wide range of undergraduate and postgraduate degrees. It's a well-respected university with a long history, and it's particularly strong in areas such as Mediterranean studies, law, and engineering. The language of instruction is primarily English, although some courses are offered in Maltese. This is a great institution.

In addition to the University of Malta, there are also a number of private colleges and institutes offering vocational courses and professional qualifications. These institutions tend to focus on specific areas, such as business, tourism, and IT. They can be a good option if you're looking for a more practical, hands-on education. The fees for private colleges and institutes vary, but they're generally lower than those for international universities. The education sector is varied.

If you're a non-EU/EEA citizen planning to study in Malta, you'll need a student visa/permit. The requirements for a student visa vary depending on your nationality and the length of your course, but generally, you'll need to provide proof of acceptance from a recognized educational institution, evidence of sufficient funds to support yourself, and health insurance. You'll also need to demonstrate that you have a genuine intention to study and that you plan to leave Malta after completing your course.

One thing to be aware of is that the Maltese education system can be quite rigid, especially in the state and church schools. There's a strong emphasis on rote learning and exams, and there's less flexibility for individual learning styles. This can be a culture shock for students who are used to a more progressive or student-centered approach. However, the system is gradually changing, and there's a growing emphasis on critical thinking and creativity.

Another challenge for expat children can be the language barrier. While English is widely spoken in Malta, the primary language of instruction in state schools is Maltese. This can make it difficult for children to follow lessons and to integrate with their classmates. Some schools offer extra support for non-Maltese speakers, but it's important to be realistic about the challenges your child might face. It can take time to adjust.

Despite the challenges, the Maltese education system offers a good standard of education, and there are options to suit every need and budget. Whether you choose a state school, a church school, or an international school, your child will receive a solid education that will prepare them for the future. And, as with everything in Malta, the experience will be enriched by the unique cultural context and the opportunity to learn a new language. It can also be fulfilling.

And now for a few practical tips for navigating the Maltese education system. Do your research and visit different schools before making a decision. Consider your child's individual needs and learning style. Be prepared for the language barrier, especially in state schools. Inquire about extra support for non-Maltese speakers. Check the school's admissions policy, fees, and waiting list.

Consider the school's location and transportation options. Get involved in the school community and meet other parents. Be patient and supportive as your child adjusts to a new school and a new culture. If you're planning to pursue higher education in Malta, research the different institutions and their courses. Check the visa requirements for non-EU/EEA students. And don't worry...you will find the education you or your child need.

Education in Malta might be a bit different from what you're used to, but it's an integral part of the Maltese experience. It's an opportunity for your children (or yourself) to learn new things, broaden their horizons, and embrace a new culture. And, who knows, they might even learn to love the Maltese language. Or, at the very least, they'll learn how to order a *pastizz* in perfect Maltese. And that, in itself, is a valuable life skill.

There is one final point which is worth raising about schools. Many working parents are simply not available to pick their kids up at 2:30 p.m., which is an issue. There is a solution, in that there is a system called Klabb 3-16, an after-school care service provided by the Foundation for Educational Services (FES). It runs throughout the school year, in the afternoons after school. The aim is to provide an inclusive and accessible after-school service that caters to children aged between 3 and 16 years.

Klabb 3-16 centers are usually located within primary schools across Malta and Gozo. This makes it convenient for parents as they can pick up their children from the same location where they attend school. The service typically operates from the end of the school day until around 6:00 pm, providing a safe and supervised environment for children during these hours. This is helpful for many parents.

The program is designed to complement the formal education system by offering a variety of activities that are both educational and recreational. These activities include homework support, arts and crafts, sports, drama, and other engaging projects. The aim is to provide a holistic development approach, promoting social skills, creativity, and physical activity. This can offer a rounded experience.

Children attending Klabb 3-16 are supervised by trained playworkers and carers. These individuals are responsible for ensuring the safety and well-being of the children, as well as facilitating the various activities. The staff-to-child ratio is maintained to ensure adequate supervision and attention for all children. This is particularly important. And the supervisors are carefully chosen.

While Klabb 3-16 is a government-subsidized service, parents are required to pay a fee. The fee structure is designed to be affordable, and there are provisions for further subsidies or exemptions for families facing financial hardship. The exact fees can vary, and it's advisable to check the latest information from the FES or the specific Klabb 3-16 center. You should contact the center or the FES.

To enroll their children in Klabb 3-16, parents typically need to fill out an application form and provide necessary documentation, such as identification and proof of residence. The registration process may also involve an interview or an orientation session to ensure that both the parents and the child are familiar with the services and expectations. It is not a complicated process, however.

Klabb 3-16 is part of a broader network of childcare services in Malta, which includes childcare centers for younger children and other after-school programs. These services aim to support working parents by providing quality care for their children outside of school hours. This is part of the government's strategy. The care is designed to be of good quality.

The service not only provides a practical solution for working parents but also contributes to the children's social and emotional development. By interacting with peers in a structured yet informal setting, children learn important social skills, cooperation, and teamwork. This will stand them in good stead in later life. It is very beneficial.

Overall, Klabb 3-16 is an integral part of Malta's efforts to support families and ensure that children have access to quality care and development opportunities outside of school hours. It reflects a commitment to balancing work and family life, recognizing the needs of modern working parents. It is a good system, well designed and expertly run. And well worth looking into.

CHAPTER SEVEN: Working in Malta: iGaming, Finance, and Finding Your Niche (Without Falling in the Sea)

Right, so you're thinking of working in Malta. Maybe you're dreaming of sipping cocktails on your lunch break, overlooking the sparkling Mediterranean. Or perhaps you envision yourself as a high-flying finance guru, raking in the euros in a sleek Valletta office. Or, more likely, you're just hoping to find a job that pays the bills and doesn't involve wearing a paper hat. Whatever your aspirations, the Maltese job market has something for (almost) everyone.

First, a reality check. While Malta's economy has been booming in recent years (again, pre-COVID caveat applies), it's not a land of endless opportunity. The job market is relatively small, and competition can be fierce, especially for non-Maltese speakers. Certain sectors are thriving, while others are, shall we say, less buoyant. And, like everywhere else, who you know can be just as important as what you know. Networking is key here.

The two big players in the Maltese job market are iGaming and finance. iGaming, or online gambling, is a massive industry in Malta, employing thousands of people, many of them expats. It's a fast-paced, dynamic sector, with companies ranging from small start-ups to multinational giants. If you have experience in areas like software development, marketing, customer support, or compliance, you'll find plenty of opportunities in iGaming. Salaries can be good, especially for skilled positions.

The finance sector is another major employer, encompassing everything from banking and insurance to fund administration and asset management. Malta has positioned itself as a financial hub, attracting international companies with its favorable tax regime and regulatory environment. If you have a background in finance, accounting, or law, you'll find a range of opportunities in Malta.

However, be prepared for a competitive job market and a demanding work culture. Competition will be tough.

Beyond iGaming and finance, there are other sectors with job opportunities. Tourism, obviously, is a major industry, although many of the jobs are seasonal and relatively low-paid. Healthcare, education, and construction also offer employment opportunities, although the salaries might not be as competitive as in iGaming or finance. There's also a growing tech scene, with a number of start-ups and established companies looking for skilled developers, designers, and project managers.

If you're a non-EU/EEA citizen, you'll need a work permit to work in Malta. As covered in Chapter Two, this usually involves securing a job offer first, and then your employer will apply for the permit on your behalf. The process can be lengthy and bureaucratic, so be prepared for a wait. EU/EEA citizens, of course, have the right to work in Malta without a permit, thanks to the freedom of movement within the EU.

The language of business in Malta is primarily English, which is a major advantage for English-speaking expats. However, knowing some Maltese can be helpful, especially if you're working in a customer-facing role or dealing with local businesses. Many companies offer Maltese language courses to their employees, and it's worth taking advantage of these if you have the opportunity. Even a few basic phrases will be appreciated by your Maltese colleagues.

The work culture in Malta can be a bit of a mixed bag. Some companies, particularly the international ones, have a very professional and structured work environment. Others, especially smaller, family-run businesses, can be more informal and relaxed. The pace of work can also vary, from the frenetic energy of an iGaming start-up to the more measured tempo of a traditional Maltese company. It's important to do your research and find a company culture that suits your personality.

One thing you'll quickly notice is that the Maltese are generally quite direct in their communication style. This can be a bit jarring for those from more reserved cultures, but it's not intended to be rude. It's just the way they communicate. Don't be afraid to ask questions and clarify anything you don't understand. It's better to be upfront than to make assumptions that could lead to misunderstandings. And misunderstandings can easily occur.

Another quirk of the Maltese work culture is the importance of relationships. Networking and building personal connections are crucial for success in Malta. It's not uncommon for jobs to be filled through word-of-mouth, and who you know can often open doors that would otherwise remain closed. So, make an effort to get to know your colleagues, attend industry events, and build your network. You never know where your next opportunity might come from.

The working hours in Malta are typically 40 hours per week, Monday to Friday. However, some industries, such as iGaming, might require longer hours or shift work. Overtime is generally paid, but it's important to clarify the terms of your employment contract before you start working. Paid annual leave is typically 25 days per year, in addition to the 14 public holidays. This is a generous allowance, and it's one of the perks of working in Malta.

Salaries in Malta can vary widely depending on the industry, the company, and your experience. Generally, salaries in iGaming and finance tend to be higher than in other sectors. However, the cost of living in Malta, especially in the popular areas, can also be quite high. It's important to do your research and negotiate a salary that allows you to live comfortably. Don't be afraid to ask for what you're worth. You deserve it.

One thing to be aware of is that Maltese employment law is generally quite favorable to employees. There are strong protections against unfair dismissal, and employers are required to provide a written contract of employment outlining the terms and conditions of your work. You're also entitled to paid sick leave, maternity leave, and other benefits. It's important to familiarize yourself with your rights as an employee.

If you're planning to start your own business in Malta, there are a number of resources available to help you. Malta Enterprise, the government agency responsible for promoting economic development, offers a range of support services for entrepreneurs, including grants, loans, and mentoring programs. There's also a growing start-up scene in Malta, with a number of incubators and accelerators providing support for new businesses. It's not too hard to start a business.

However, starting a business in Malta is not without its challenges. The bureaucracy can be daunting, and the market is relatively small. It's important to do your research, develop a solid business plan, and seek advice from experienced entrepreneurs. There are numerous networking events and workshops for start-ups in Malta, and these can be a valuable source of information and support. Don't give up on your dream. It can be done.

One of the advantages of working in Malta is the opportunity to live in a beautiful Mediterranean island with a rich history and culture. The weather is generally fantastic, the beaches are stunning, and the lifestyle is relaxed. It's a great place to raise a family, and there are plenty of activities and attractions to keep you entertained. However, it's important to remember that Malta is not a holiday destination. It's a place to live and work.

You'll encounter the same challenges and frustrations as you would anywhere else, from traffic congestion to bureaucratic delays. You'll also need to adapt to the Maltese way of life, which can be quite different from what you're used to. But if you're willing to embrace the challenges and learn to appreciate the quirks, working in Malta can be a rewarding experience. You might even find yourself falling in love with this quirky little island.

And now for a few tips, to help your job hunt go well. Research the Maltese job market and identify the sectors that are most relevant to your skills and experience. Tailor your CV and cover letter to the Maltese market, highlighting your relevant skills and experience. Use online job portals, such as LinkedIn, Indeed, and MaltaPark, to search for jobs. Contact recruitment agencies specializing in the Maltese market. Network with people in your industry and attend industry events.

Be prepared for a competitive job market and don't be discouraged by rejections. Learn some basic Maltese phrases to show your interest in the local culture. Familiarize yourself with Maltese employment law and your rights as an employee. Negotiate your salary and benefits package carefully. Be patient and persistent, and don't give up on your job search. If you're starting a business, do your research, develop a solid business plan, and seek advice from experienced entrepreneurs.

Consider joining a co-working space to meet other professionals and entrepreneurs. Malta has a thriving digital nomad community, and there are numerous co-working spaces offering flexible workspaces, networking opportunities, and social events. These spaces can be a great way to meet other expats, share experiences, and build your professional network. They can also be a good option if you're working remotely or freelancing. Look into them.

If you're looking for a more traditional office environment, there are also a number of serviced offices available in Malta. These offices provide fully furnished and equipped workspaces, with reception services, meeting rooms, and other amenities. They can be a good option if you need a professional space to work but don't want to commit to a long-term lease. The prices for serviced offices vary depending on the location and the facilities.

One thing to consider when choosing a workplace is the commute. Traffic in Malta can be heavy, especially during peak hours, and public transport can be unreliable. If you're living in one of the central areas, such as Sliema or St. Julian's, it's often easier to walk or cycle to work than to drive. If you're living further out, you might need to factor in a longer commute time. Be prepared for potential delays.

Another thing to consider is the work-life balance. While the Maltese generally work hard, they also value their leisure time. It's not uncommon for people to take long lunch breaks, especially in the summer, and to socialize with colleagues after work. There's a strong emphasis on family and community, and people generally prioritize spending time with their loved ones. It's a more relaxed approach to life than in some other countries.

If you're used to a fast-paced, high-pressure work environment, you might find the Maltese pace of life a bit slow at first. But it's important to adapt to the local culture and to respect the Maltese way of doing things. Don't try to impose your own work style on your colleagues, and be open to learning new ways of working. You might even find that you appreciate the more relaxed approach. Embrace it.

Working in Malta can be a challenging, but ultimately rewarding, experience. It's an opportunity to develop your career, learn new skills, and live in a beautiful and unique environment. You'll encounter new challenges, meet new people, and discover a new culture. And, who knows, you might even learn to love the Maltese way of life. Or, at the very least, you'll learn how to order a *Kinnie* and a *pastizz* like a pro.

One thing that is worth being prepared for, however, is the slower pace of many things in Malta. Things happen slower here. It is very important to understand this, or you may become frustrated. And it is pointless becoming frustrated by it - as it is part of Maltese culture. So you need to get used to it - or you will be pulling your hair out, a hair-pulling experience which will serve no purpose at all.

Embrace the Maltese way, and things will be fine. Go against the grain however, and you will not enjoy your new life. Living and working in Malta can be a success if you do things the Maltese way - which may well be very different to what you are used to. Do not expect things to be done the same way as you are used to in your home country. They will not be. Expect things to be different.

CHAPTER EIGHT: The Cost of Living: Is it Cheaper Than Your Ex's Therapy Bills?

Alright, let's talk money. You've probably heard whispers of Malta being a "low-cost" destination. Maybe you've seen articles touting its affordable lifestyle and tax benefits. Or perhaps you've just assumed that anything smaller than Rhode Island must be cheap. Well, prepare for a reality check. While Malta *can* be more affordable than some Western European countries, it's not exactly a budget traveler's paradise. It all depends on your lifestyle, your spending habits, and your ability to resist the siren call of those delicious, but surprisingly pricey, *pastizzi*.

Think of Malta's cost of living as a rollercoaster. There are ups, downs, and unexpected loops that can leave your wallet feeling a bit queasy. Some things are surprisingly affordable, like public transport and certain groceries. Others, like rent and imported goods, can be eye-wateringly expensive. The key is to understand the cost landscape and to budget accordingly. And, perhaps, to develop a taste for local beer instead of imported craft IPAs. It is essential to be aware of the details.

Let's start with the big one: housing. As mentioned in Chapter Three, rent in Malta, especially in the popular areas like Sliema and St. Julian's, has skyrocketed in recent years. You can expect to pay a premium for anything with a sea view, a balcony, or even just a functioning air conditioner. A decent one-bedroom apartment in a central location can easily set you back €800-€1,200 per month, or even more. Two-bedroom apartments typically start around €1,000 and can go up to €2,000 or higher, depending on the location and amenities.

If you're on a tighter budget, you'll need to look further afield. Towns like Mellieha, Bugibba, and Qawra in the north, or Marsaskala and Birzebbuga in the south, offer more affordable options. You might be able to find a one-bedroom apartment for €600-€800 per month, or a two-bedroom for €800-€1,000.

However, you'll need to factor in the longer commute times to the main business hubs. And there will, naturally, be fewer facilities available.

Gozo, Malta's sister island, is generally more affordable than Malta, with rents typically 20-30% lower. However, you'll need to factor in the ferry commute to Malta if you plan to work there. The ferry itself is relatively inexpensive, but the journey can take an hour or more, depending on the weather and the traffic. It's a trade-off between affordability and convenience. So it is up to you to decide.

Utility bills in Malta can also be surprisingly high, especially in the summer. Electricity is the main culprit, thanks to the widespread use of air conditioning. Expect to pay €100-€200 per month for electricity during the summer months, and potentially even more if you have a large apartment or a penchant for keeping your AC on full blast 24/7. Water is also relatively expensive, although the bills are generally lower than electricity. Water costs normally come to around €50 per month.

Internet and mobile phone services are reasonably priced, with a range of providers offering competitive packages. You can get a decent broadband connection for around €30-€40 per month, and a mobile phone plan with unlimited calls and data for a similar price. However, be aware that the internet speed and reliability can vary depending on your location. Some areas have excellent fiber-optic connections, while others are still stuck with slower ADSL technology.

Groceries in Malta can be a mixed bag. Local produce, such as fruit, vegetables, and bread, is generally affordable, especially if you buy from local markets or street vendors. Imported goods, however, can be significantly more expensive than in other European countries. This is due to the cost of shipping everything to a small island. Expect to pay a premium for your favorite brands of cereal, coffee, and chocolate. So you will pay a premium for comfort food.

There are several supermarket chains in Malta, including Lidl, Pavi, Pama, Scotts, and Wellbees. Lidl is generally considered to be the cheapest option, offering a range of discount products. Pavi and Pama are larger supermarkets with a wider selection of goods, including imported items. Scotts and Wellbees are more upmarket supermarkets, offering a range of gourmet and specialty products. The prices vary accordingly, so it's worth shopping around to find the best deals.

Eating out in Malta can range from incredibly cheap to surprisingly expensive, depending on where you go. A *pastizz*, the traditional Maltese savory pastry, will only set you back a few cents, and you can get a decent pizza or pasta dish for €8-€12. However, if you're dining in a fancy restaurant in Valletta or St. Julian's, expect to pay significantly more. A three-course meal for two with wine can easily cost €80-€100, or even higher.

There are plenty of affordable options for eating out in Malta, especially if you're willing to venture beyond the tourist hotspots. Local *ftira*, a type of Maltese bread filled with various ingredients, is a popular and inexpensive lunch option. You can also find numerous small cafes and kiosks selling sandwiches, wraps, and salads for a few euros. And, of course, there's always the option of cooking at home, which is generally the most budget-friendly approach.

Public transport in Malta is surprisingly affordable, with a single bus ticket costing €2 in summer and €1.50 in winter. You can also buy a weekly or monthly pass, which offers even better value if you use the bus frequently. The bus network is extensive, covering most parts of Malta and Gozo, but it can be unreliable, especially during peak hours. Buses are often crowded, and they can get stuck in traffic, especially in the central areas.

Taxis are readily available in Malta, but they're significantly more expensive than the bus. A short taxi ride can easily cost €10-€15, and longer journeys can be much pricier. There are also several ride-hailing apps operating in Malta, such as Bolt and eCabs, which offer a more convenient and often cheaper alternative to traditional taxis. However, be aware that surge pricing can apply during peak hours or in areas with high demand.

If you're planning to drive in Malta, you'll need to factor in the cost of car insurance, fuel, and parking. Car insurance is mandatory, and the premiums can vary depending on your age, your driving history, and the type of car you drive. Fuel prices are generally in line with European averages, but they can fluctuate depending on global oil prices. Parking can be a challenge in Malta, especially in the central areas. Paid parking is not always available, or cheap.

One of the perks of living in Malta is the relatively low tax rate. The income tax system is progressive, with rates ranging from 0% to 35%. However, there are a number of tax deductions and credits available, which can significantly reduce your tax burden. If you're employed, your employer will deduct tax from your salary each month under the Final Settlement System (FSS). If you're self-employed, you'll need to file an annual tax return and pay your taxes directly to the Inland Revenue Department.

Malta also has a number of tax incentives for expats, particularly those working in certain sectors or investing in the country. These incentives can significantly reduce your tax burden, but it's important to seek professional advice to ensure that you're complying with all the rules and regulations. There are numerous tax advisors and accountants in Malta who specialize in expat tax matters. It is worth consulting with these professionals.

Healthcare in Malta, as discussed in Chapter Five, is a mix of public and private options. The public system is free or very low-cost for legal residents, but it can involve long waiting times. Private health insurance is a popular option for expats, as it provides access to faster and more personalized care. The cost of private health insurance varies depending on your age, your health status, and the level of coverage you choose.

Entertainment and leisure activities in Malta can range from free to expensive, depending on your preferences. Swimming in the sea, sunbathing on the beach, and exploring the historical sites are all free or low-cost activities. There are also numerous free events and festivals throughout the year, such as village *festas* and cultural performances. However, if you're into fine dining, clubbing, or water sports, you'll need to budget accordingly. It all depends on your taste.

A night out in Paceville, Malta's main nightlife district, can easily set you back €50-€100, or even more, depending on your drinking habits. Water sports, such as diving, jet skiing, and boat trips, can also be quite expensive. However, there are plenty of affordable options for entertainment, such as going to the cinema, visiting museums, or attending local concerts and performances. It's all about finding a balance that suits your budget and your interests.

So, is Malta cheaper than your ex's therapy bills? It depends. If you're living a frugal lifestyle, cooking most of your meals at home, using public transport, and avoiding the tourist traps, you can probably live quite comfortably on a relatively modest budget. However, if you're living in a central location, eating out frequently, and enjoying all the entertainment that Malta has to offer, you'll need a significantly higher income. And, even then, it still might be cheaper than the therapy...

And now for a few more practical tips, to manage your budget in Malta. Shop around for the best deals on groceries, utilities, and insurance. Take advantage of free or low-cost activities, such as swimming, hiking, and exploring historical sites. Use public transport or cycling instead of driving whenever possible. Cook at home instead of eating out frequently. Set a budget and track your expenses to avoid overspending.

Consider living in a more affordable area, even if it means a longer commute. Take advantage of tax deductions and credits to reduce your tax burden. Look for free events and festivals to enjoy entertainment on a budget. Don't be afraid to negotiate prices, especially for rent and long-term services. And learn to love *pastizzi*. They're cheap, delicious, and a true Maltese staple. Just don't eat *too* many, or you'll need to budget for a new wardrobe.

The cost of living in Malta is a complex equation with many variables. It's not as cheap as some people might think, but it's also not as expensive as some of the pricier European capitals. It all comes down to your lifestyle, your spending habits, and your ability to adapt to the local way of life. And, perhaps, your willingness to embrace the occasional *pastizz*-induced food coma. After all, you're living in Malta now. Embrace the chaos, enjoy the sunshine, and try not to let your bank balance give you an ulcer.

One thing to be aware of is that many things that are cheap elsewhere are not cheap in Malta. For example stationery, printer cartridges, books, clothes, and small electrical goods tend to be more expensive. This is a result of Malta's island status, which has been previously mentioned. But this fact does affect the cost of living. So if you are able to stock up on these items before moving to Malta, it might be well worth doing so.

Likewise, services, and people's time are valued and charged for. So you may be pleasantly surprised in this respect. Some things may be cheaper, which helps to balance out the things which are more expensive. For this reason it is difficult to definitively answer the question "is it cheaper than my ex's therapy bills?". Only you will be able to answer that question. But at least this chapter has given you some factors to consider.

One final consideration is the cost of setting up. Be prepared for paying a deposit and a month's rent. And be prepared to have to buy furniture if your place is not furnished. So it is important to factor that cost into your considerations when you move to Malta. There may well be other costs which come as a surprise, but that is true of moving anywhere. The general idea of this chapter is to help you to be aware of as many of these things as possible.

Overall it is fair to say that the cost of living in Malta is neither particularly cheap, nor is it particularly expensive. It is somewhere in between. And it can be less expensive than many other places in Europe. But a lot depends on how you live your life, as has been pointed out. It is best to be aware of all of these things before you arrive, so there are as few surprises as possible.

CHAPTER NINE: Transport: Buses, Boats, and Braving the Roundabouts of Doom

Okay, you've made it this far. You're legally residing in Malta, you have a roof over your head, money in the bank, access to healthcare, maybe even a job or a school for the kids. Now, you need to get around. And this, my friend, is where the *real* Maltese adventure begins. Forget the ancient temples and the stunning beaches; navigating Malta's transport system is a cultural experience in itself. It's a chaotic, occasionally terrifying, but ultimately rewarding journey.

Think of Maltese transport as a three-ring circus. In the first ring, you have the buses: lumbering yellow beasts that are the backbone of the public transport system. In the second ring, you have the ferries: a vital link between Malta, Gozo, and Comino. And in the third ring, the main attraction, you have the cars: a swirling, honking mass of metal that seems to operate under a unique set of rules, best described as "organized chaos."

Let's start with the buses. Malta Public Transport (MPT) operates a network of routes covering most of the island. The buses are generally modern and air-conditioned (a lifesaver in the summer), and they're surprisingly affordable. As mentioned before, a single ticket costs €2 in summer and €1.50 in winter, and you can buy multi-day passes for even better value. The routes and timetables are available online and on the Tallinja app, which also offers real-time tracking of buses.

Sounds good, right? Well, here's the catch. The buses are often late, sometimes crowded, and occasionally, they simply don't show up at all. This is partly due to traffic congestion, especially in the central areas, and partly due to the, shall we say, *relaxed* approach to timekeeping that's characteristic of Maltese culture. If you're used to the punctual precision of Swiss trains or German buses, you're in for a shock. You will have to be patient.

The bus drivers themselves are a breed apart. They're generally skilled drivers, navigating the narrow, winding streets with impressive dexterity. But they're also known for their, um, *assertive* driving style. They're not afraid to honk their horns, squeeze through impossibly tight gaps, and occasionally, bend the rules of the road. If you're a nervous passenger, you might want to close your eyes and pray to your deity of choice.

Despite the challenges, the bus system is a viable option for getting around Malta, especially if you're on a budget or don't want to deal with the stress of driving. It's a great way to see the island, and you'll get a glimpse of local life that you wouldn't get from a taxi or a rental car. Just be prepared for the occasional delay, the crowded conditions, and the, shall we say, *spirited* driving style of the bus drivers.

Now, let's move on to the ferries. If you're planning to visit Gozo or Comino, you'll need to take a ferry. The Gozo Channel Company operates a regular service between Cirkewwa in Malta and Mgarr in Gozo. The ferries run frequently throughout the day, and the journey takes about 25 minutes. The fare is very reasonable, especially if you're traveling as a foot passenger. You can also take your car on the ferry, but it's more expensive and you might have to wait in line, especially during peak season.

The ferry journey itself is quite pleasant, offering stunning views of the coastline and the clear blue waters of the Mediterranean. It's a great way to escape the hustle and bustle of Malta and experience the more relaxed pace of life on Gozo. However, be aware that the sea can get rough, especially during the winter months. If you're prone to seasickness, you might want to take some medication before you board. Also, be ready for delays and cancellations.

There's also a fast ferry service between Valletta and Mgarr (Gozo), which takes about 45 minutes. This is a more convenient option if you're staying in Valletta or the surrounding areas, but it's also more expensive than the Cirkewwa-Mgarr ferry. The fast ferry is primarily for foot passengers, although it can also accommodate a limited number of bicycles. It's a modern, comfortable vessel, and the journey is generally smooth and enjoyable.

Comino, the tiny island famous for its Blue Lagoon, is also accessible by ferry. There are several small boats operating from Cirkewwa and Marfa in Malta, and from Mgarr in Gozo. The journey to Comino is short, taking only about 15-20 minutes, but the boats can get crowded, especially during the summer months. It's a popular destination for day-trippers, and the Blue Lagoon can get very busy, especially during peak season.

If you're planning to visit Comino, it's best to go early in the morning or late in the afternoon to avoid the crowds. You can also explore the rest of the island, which is mostly uninhabited and offers some stunning scenery and hiking trails. Just be aware that there are limited facilities on Comino, so bring your own food and water, and wear appropriate footwear. And, of course, don't forget your sunscreen. It's the Mediterranean after all.

And now, the main event: driving in Malta. Buckle up, because this is where things get *really* interesting. Driving in Malta is not for the faint of heart. It's a chaotic, exhilarating, and occasionally terrifying experience, requiring nerves of steel, quick reflexes, and a healthy dose of fatalism. Think of it as a real-life video game, where the obstacles are roundabouts, the power-ups are parking spaces, and the final boss is the Maltese driving test.

The first thing you need to know about driving in Malta is that they drive on the left, like in the UK, Australia, and a few other former British colonies. This can be a challenge for drivers from countries where they drive on the right, but you'll get used to it eventually. Just remember to keep left, especially when approaching roundabouts. And, trust us, you'll be approaching a *lot* of roundabouts. The Maltese love the things.

Roundabouts are the defining feature of the Maltese road system. They're everywhere, from the tiny village squares to the major arterial roads. And they're the source of much confusion, frustration, and near-miss accidents for expat drivers. The rules of the roundabout are, in theory, simple: give way to traffic already on the roundabout, and signal your exit. In practice, however, Maltese roundabouts operate under a different set of rules, best described as "survival of the fittest."

You'll encounter drivers entering the roundabout without yielding, exiting from the wrong lane, and generally ignoring all the rules of the road. You'll need to be assertive, but not aggressive, and you'll need to anticipate the unpredictable behavior of other drivers. It's a constant game of cat and mouse, where the stakes are your car's bodywork and your sanity. But, with practice, you'll learn to navigate the roundabouts of doom.

Another challenge of driving in Malta is the narrow, winding streets, especially in the older towns and villages. You'll encounter roads that are barely wide enough for two cars to pass, let alone park. You'll need to be skilled at maneuvering in tight spaces, and you'll need to be patient, as you'll often encounter traffic jams and delays. Parking is also a major issue, especially in the central areas. Finding a parking space can feel like winning the lottery.

Despite the challenges, driving in Malta can be a rewarding experience. It gives you the freedom to explore the island at your own pace, and it allows you to access areas that are difficult to reach by public transport. You'll discover hidden beaches, charming villages, and stunning viewpoints that you would otherwise miss. Just be prepared for the chaos, the narrow streets, and the, um, *creative* driving style of the Maltese. It's all part of the adventure.

If you're planning to drive in Malta, you'll need a valid driving license. If you have an EU/EEA license, you can use it in Malta without any restrictions. If you have a license from a non-EU/EEA country, you can use it for up to 12 months, after which you'll need to exchange it for a Maltese license. The process of exchanging your license involves filling out a form, providing some documents, and passing a practical driving test.

The Maltese driving test is notoriously difficult, and many expats fail it on their first attempt. It's not just about your driving skills; it's also about your knowledge of the Maltese Highway Code and your ability to navigate the unique challenges of Maltese roads. You'll be tested on your ability to handle roundabouts, your observation skills, and your overall awareness of other road users. It's a stressful experience, but it's also a rite of passage for expat drivers.

Once you have a Maltese driving license, you'll need to register your car and pay the annual circulation tax. The amount of tax you pay depends on the age and emissions of your car. You'll also need to have car insurance, which is mandatory in Malta. There are several insurance providers offering a range of policies, from basic third-party coverage to comprehensive insurance that covers all types of damage. It's important to compare the different policies and choose one that meets your needs and budget.

One thing to be aware of is that car theft and vandalism are not uncommon in Malta, especially in the more touristy areas. It's important to take precautions, such as parking in well-lit areas, not leaving valuables in your car, and considering installing an alarm system. It's also a good idea to have comprehensive car insurance that covers theft and vandalism. Prevention is, of course, better than cure.

Another challenge of driving in Malta is the sheer volume of traffic, especially during peak hours. The roads can get very congested, especially in the central areas, and journey times can be significantly longer than expected. It's important to factor in extra time for your journeys, especially if you're driving to the airport or an important appointment. And be prepared for the occasional traffic jam. They happen all the time, sadly.

Despite the challenges, driving in Malta can be a rewarding experience. It gives you the freedom to explore the island at your own pace, and it allows you to access areas that are difficult to reach by public transport. You'll discover hidden beaches, charming villages, and stunning viewpoints that you would otherwise miss. Just be prepared for the chaos, the narrow streets, and the, um, *creative* driving style of the Maltese.

And now for a few driving tips, to help you to navigate the Maltese roads. Always drive on the left, and give way to traffic already on roundabouts. Be assertive, but not aggressive, and anticipate the unpredictable behavior of other drivers. Be prepared for narrow streets, traffic jams, and parking challenges. Get a good map or GPS navigation system, and familiarize yourself with the main roads and landmarks.

Learn some basic Maltese phrases related to driving, such as "*Fejn hi l-eqreb parkeġġ?*" (Where is the nearest parking lot?). Take a defensive driving course to improve your skills and awareness. Avoid driving during peak hours if possible. Consider renting a small car, as it will be easier to maneuver in tight spaces. And don't be afraid to ask for directions if you get lost. The Maltese are generally helpful and friendly.

Malta's transport system is a microcosm of Maltese culture: chaotic, colorful, and full of surprises. Whether you're braving the buses, navigating the ferries, or taking on the roundabouts of doom, you're in for an adventure. It's not always easy, but it's never boring. And, ultimately, it's a rewarding experience that will give you a unique perspective on this quirky little island. Just remember to keep your sense of humor, your patience, and your wits about you.

One final point about the roundabouts. They are an essential part of driving in Malta, and so mastering them is essential. And part of this is understanding which lane you should be in, when approaching and exiting. As a general rule, to turn left or go straight, you should approach in the left-hand lane; and to turn right, you should approach in the right hand lane.

Do not be afraid to go round again if you end up in the wrong lane. This is better than making a dangerous maneuver. And if you do make a dangerous maneuver, you might well get a loud blast of the horn from other Maltese drivers. Which brings us on to the final point about driving in Malta: the Maltese use of the horn. They use it more than other nationalities.

If you make a mistake, even a minor one, do not be surprised if you get a blast of the horn. And it will be loud. Do not take offense at this. It is just the Maltese way. And you might even find yourself using your own horn in this way, after a while. In fact, if you *don't* find yourself doing this, you are probably not integrating into Maltese life.

CHAPTER TEN: Maltese Culture: Embrace the Chaos (and the *Pastizzi*)

Alright, you've survived the bureaucracy, the housing hunt, the banking maze, and the transport rollercoaster. Now, it's time to immerse yourself in Maltese culture. And, *mela*, it's a wild ride. Think of it as a vibrant, chaotic tapestry woven from threads of Mediterranean passion, Arabic influence, British pragmatism, and a healthy dose of "anything goes." It's loud, it's colorful, it's occasionally baffling, and it's utterly unique.

The first thing you'll notice about the Maltese is their warmth and hospitality. They're generally welcoming of foreigners, especially those who make an effort to understand and appreciate their culture. They're proud of their heritage, their traditions, and their tiny island nation, and they're usually happy to share it with newcomers. Don't be surprised if you're invited to a family gathering, a village *festa*, or just a casual coffee with someone you've just met.

However, the Maltese can also be quite direct in their communication style, which can sometimes be misinterpreted as rudeness by those from more reserved cultures. They're not afraid to express their opinions, to argue passionately about politics or football, or to tell you exactly what they think of your driving. It's not personal; it's just the way they communicate. Don't take offense, and don't be afraid to engage in a bit of lively debate.

Family is incredibly important in Maltese society. You'll often see multiple generations living together or gathering for large family meals. Sundays are traditionally a family day, with many people attending church in the morning and then spending the afternoon with their relatives. Family ties are strong, and loyalty to family is paramount. This can be a bit overwhelming for expats who are used to a more individualistic culture, but it's also one of the most endearing aspects of Maltese life.

Religion also plays a significant role in Maltese culture, with the vast majority of the population identifying as Roman Catholic. Churches are everywhere, and they're not just for Sundays. You'll hear church bells ringing throughout the day, and you'll see religious statues and shrines on street corners and in homes. Religious holidays are major events, and the village *festas*, held in honor of patron saints, are a vibrant expression of Maltese faith and tradition.

The *festas* are a must-see for any expat. They're a week-long celebration of a village's patron saint, with fireworks, processions, band marches, and plenty of food and drink. The streets are decorated with colorful lights and banners, and the atmosphere is electric. It's a noisy, chaotic, and utterly joyful experience, and it's a great way to immerse yourself in Maltese culture. Just be prepared for late nights and a lot of fireworks.

The Maltese love of fireworks is legendary. They're not just for *festas*; they're used to celebrate any and every occasion, from weddings and birthdays to football victories and political rallies. The fireworks displays can be spectacular, with elaborate creations that light up the night sky. However, they can also be incredibly loud, and they can go on for hours. If you're a light sleeper, you might want to invest in some earplugs.

Food is another central element of Maltese culture. The cuisine is a delicious blend of Mediterranean, Arabic, and Italian influences, with a focus on fresh, seasonal ingredients. *Pastizzi*, the flaky pastries filled with ricotta or peas, are the national snack, and you'll find them everywhere. Other traditional dishes include *fenek* (rabbit stew), *lampuki* (a type of fish), and *stuffat tal-qarnit* (octopus stew). The portions are generally generous, and the food is meant to be shared.

Eating out is a popular pastime in Malta, and there are restaurants and cafes to suit every taste and budget. The Maltese love to socialize over food and drink, and meals can be long, leisurely affairs. Don't be surprised if you're offered a complimentary *digestivo*, a strong liqueur, after your meal. It's a Maltese tradition, and it's considered rude to refuse. Just be warned: some of them are *very* strong. Pace yourself!

The Maltese are also passionate about their language. Maltese is a Semitic language with roots in Arabic, Italian, and English. It's a unique and fascinating language, and it's the only Semitic language written in the Latin alphabet. While English is widely spoken, especially in the tourist areas and in business, learning a few basic Maltese phrases will be greatly appreciated by the locals. It shows that you're making an effort to understand and appreciate their culture.

The Maltese sense of time is, shall we say, *flexible*. Things don't always happen on schedule, and punctuality is not always a priority. This can be frustrating for expats who are used to a more structured and organized way of life, but it's part of the Maltese charm. Learn to relax, go with the flow, and embrace the "mañana" attitude. Things will get done eventually, just maybe not as quickly as you'd expect.

The Maltese are also known for their love of a good bargain. Haggling is common in markets and small shops, and it's considered perfectly acceptable to try to negotiate a lower price. Don't be afraid to try your luck, but be polite and respectful. It's all part of the game, and it can be a fun way to interact with the locals. Just don't expect to get a huge discount; the Maltese are shrewd negotiators.

One of the most endearing aspects of Maltese culture is the strong sense of community. In the villages, especially, people know their neighbors, and they look out for each other. There's a sense of belonging and a shared identity that's hard to find in many other parts of the world. This can be a great comfort for expats, especially those who are feeling homesick or isolated. Don't be afraid to reach out to your neighbors and get involved in local events.

The Maltese are also fiercely proud of their history and their heritage. The islands have been inhabited for over 7,000 years, and they've been ruled by a succession of different powers, from the Phoenicians and the Romans to the Knights of St. John and the British. This rich history is reflected in the architecture, the language, and the traditions of the Maltese people. Take the time to explore the historical sites and learn about the island's fascinating past.

One of the challenges for expats can be adapting to the slower pace of life. Things move more slowly in Malta, and it can take time to get things done. Bureaucracy can be slow and frustrating, and appointments are often delayed or rescheduled. It's important to be patient and to adjust your expectations. Don't try to rush things; it will only lead to frustration. Embrace the slower pace, and learn to enjoy the simple pleasures of life.

Another challenge can be the noise. Malta is a densely populated island, and it can be quite noisy, especially in the urban areas. You'll hear traffic, construction, church bells, fireworks, and the constant chatter of people talking and laughing. If you're sensitive to noise, you might want to consider living in a quieter area, such as a village or a rural part of the island. Or invest in some good noise-canceling headphones.

Despite the challenges, Maltese culture is warm, welcoming, and utterly unique. It's a blend of old and new, traditional and modern, chaotic and charming. It's a culture that values family, community, and tradition, but it's also open to new influences and new ideas. It's a culture that will challenge your preconceptions, broaden your horizons, and probably leave you with a lifelong love of *pastizzi*.

The Maltese are generally quite informal in their social interactions. They're not big on formalities or strict etiquette. First names are commonly used, even in business settings, and greetings are usually warm and friendly. However, it's still considered polite to address older people or those in positions of authority with "Mr." or "Mrs." followed by their surname, unless they invite you to use their first name.

Public displays of affection are common in Malta. You'll often see couples holding hands, kissing, and hugging in public. It's not considered inappropriate or offensive, and it's just a reflection of the warm and affectionate nature of the Maltese people. However, excessive displays of affection, especially in religious settings, are frowned upon. It's all about finding a balance between being affectionate and being respectful.

The Maltese are generally quite tolerant and accepting of different lifestyles and beliefs. However, they're also quite traditional in some ways, and they value family and community above all else. Homosexuality is legal in Malta, and same-sex marriage was legalized in 2017. However, public opinion on LGBTQ+ issues is still evolving, and some people, especially older generations, may hold more conservative views.

Dress codes in Malta are generally quite relaxed. Casual wear is acceptable in most settings, although it's considered polite to dress more formally for business meetings and special occasions. When visiting churches, it's important to dress modestly, covering your shoulders and knees. Shorts, tank tops, and revealing clothing are generally frowned upon in religious settings. It's a sign of respect for the local culture and traditions.

Tipping is customary in Malta, although it's not as widespread or as generous as in some other countries. In restaurants, a tip of 5-10% is considered appropriate, depending on the service. It's also customary to tip taxi drivers, hairdressers, and other service providers, although the amount is usually smaller. Rounding up the bill to the nearest euro is a common practice. It's not obligatory, but it's a sign of appreciation for good service.

The Maltese are generally quite punctual for social events, although they might be a bit more relaxed about business appointments. If you're invited to someone's home for dinner, it's considered polite to arrive on time or a few minutes late. Arriving early is considered a bit odd, as your hosts might still be preparing. Bringing a small gift, such as a bottle of wine or some flowers, is a nice gesture, but it's not expected.

The Maltese are known for their hospitality, and they'll often go out of their way to make you feel welcome. If you're invited to a Maltese home, you'll likely be offered food and drink, even if you're just visiting for a short time. It's considered rude to refuse, so be prepared to eat and drink, even if you're not hungry or thirsty. It's all part of the Maltese way of showing hospitality and making you feel at home.

The Maltese love to celebrate, and there are numerous festivals and events throughout the year. In addition to the village *festas*, there are also national holidays, such as Independence Day (September 21st), Republic Day (December 13th), and Freedom Day (March 31st). These holidays are celebrated with parades, fireworks, and other festivities. There are also numerous cultural events, such as the Malta Arts Festival, the Malta Jazz Festival, and the Notte Bianca, a night-time celebration of arts and culture.

One of the best ways to experience Maltese culture is to simply wander around the streets and observe the everyday life of the locals. Visit the local markets, chat with the shopkeepers, and sit in a cafe and watch the world go by. You'll learn more about Maltese culture from these simple interactions than you ever could from a guidebook. And you'll probably make some new friends along the way.

Maltese culture is a vibrant, chaotic, and utterly unique blend of influences. It's a culture that values family, community, tradition, and hospitality. It's a culture that will challenge your preconceptions, broaden your horizons, and probably leave you with a lifelong love of *pastizzi*, fireworks, and a slightly more relaxed approach to timekeeping. Embrace the chaos, enjoy the warmth, and get ready for an unforgettable cultural experience.

One of the things that often surprises expats is the Maltese sense of humor. It can be quite dry, sarcastic, and self-deprecating. The Maltese love to laugh, and they're not afraid to make fun of themselves or their situations. They often use humor to diffuse tense situations or to express their opinions in a subtle way. Don't be offended if a Maltese person makes a joke at your expense; it's usually meant in good humor.

Another aspect of Maltese culture that's worth mentioning is the concept of "*pika*." *Pika* is a Maltese word that roughly translates to "rivalry" or "competition." It can manifest itself in various ways, from friendly banter between football fans to intense competition between villages during *festas*. It's a complex concept that's deeply ingrained in Maltese society, and it can be both a source of amusement and a cause of conflict.

Pika is often seen between neighboring villages, especially during *festa* time. Each village wants to have the best fireworks display, the most elaborate decorations, and the most impressive procession. This rivalry can be quite intense, and it can lead to some creative and sometimes outrageous displays of one-upmanship. It's all part of the fun, and it's a testament to the Maltese passion and competitive spirit.

Pika can also be seen in politics, business, and even everyday life. The Maltese are generally quite competitive, and they like to be the best at whatever they do. This can be a positive thing, as it drives them to achieve great things. But it can also lead to jealousy, resentment, and sometimes, even conflict. It's a double-edged sword, and it's an integral part of the Maltese character.

Despite the *pika* and the occasional disagreements, the Maltese are generally a very close-knit community. They value their relationships with family and friends, and they're always willing to help each other out. There's a strong sense of solidarity, especially in times of need. This sense of community is one of the things that makes Malta such a special place to live.

So, embrace the chaos, the warmth, the directness, the *festas*, the fireworks, the food, the language, the flexible sense of time, the haggling, the community spirit, the history, the *pika*, and, of course, the *pastizzi*. Maltese culture is a rich and rewarding experience that will stay with you long after you've left the island.

It's a culture that will challenge you, surprise you, and ultimately, make you feel like you belong.

CHAPTER ELEVEN: Learning Maltese: *Mela*, You Don't *Have* To, But It Helps

Right, let's address the elephant in the room, or rather, the *iljunfant fil-kamra* (that's Maltese for "elephant in the room," in case you were wondering). Are you going to learn Maltese? *Mela*, you don't *have* to. English is an official language, and it's widely spoken, especially in the tourist areas and in business. You can get by perfectly well without uttering a single word of Maltese. But... where's the fun in that?

Think of learning Maltese as an optional side quest in your expat adventure. It's not essential for survival, but it adds a whole new dimension to the experience. It's like unlocking a secret level in a video game, where you discover hidden pathways, Easter eggs, and a deeper understanding of the game's mechanics. Plus, it's a great way to impress the locals, confuse your friends back home, and maybe even order a *pastizz* without resorting to pointing and grunting.

Let's be honest, Maltese is not the easiest language to learn. It's a Semitic language, related to Arabic, Hebrew, and Aramaic, but with a heavy dose of Italian and English vocabulary thrown in for good measure. It sounds like nothing else you've ever heard, and the grammar can be, shall we say, *challenging*. It's a linguistic puzzle, a verbal Rubik's Cube, and a testament to Malta's complex and fascinating history.

The first thing that will strike you about Maltese is its sound. It's full of guttural sounds, throaty consonants, and vowel combinations that will make your tongue twist in ways you never thought possible. The most infamous sound is the "għ," which is represented by the letter "għajn" (meaning "eye"). It's a silent letter, but it affects the pronunciation of the surrounding vowels, creating a subtle but distinct sound that's notoriously difficult for non-native speakers to master.

Then there's the "q," which is not the "kw" sound you're used to in English. It's a glottal stop, a brief pause in the airflow, like the sound you make in the middle of "uh-oh." It's a subtle sound, but it's crucial for distinguishing between words like "*qattus*" (cat) and "*katus*" (cactus). Getting it right takes practice, and you'll probably sound a bit like you're choking at first, but don't worry, the Maltese are used to it.

The grammar of Maltese is another beast altogether. It's based on Arabic grammar, which is quite different from the grammar of English or other European languages. Verbs are conjugated according to person, number, and gender, and they change depending on the tense and the mood. There are also different forms of verbs depending on whether the action is completed or ongoing. It's a complex system, and it takes time and effort to master.

Nouns also have genders, masculine and feminine, and they change their form depending on whether they're singular or plural. There are also different forms of nouns depending on whether they're definite (preceded by the article "il-") or indefinite (without the article). And, of course, there are exceptions to every rule, because why make things easy? It's a grammatical minefield, but it's also fascinating to see how it all works.

Despite the challenges, learning Maltese can be a rewarding experience. It's a way to connect with the local culture, to understand the nuances of Maltese humor, and to gain a deeper appreciation for the island's history and traditions. It's also a great way to exercise your brain and to challenge yourself to learn something new. And, let's face it, it's pretty cool to be able to speak a language that only a few hundred thousand people in the world understand.

If you're serious about learning Maltese, there are several options available. You can take classes at a language school, hire a private tutor, or use online resources and language learning apps. There are also several Maltese language courses offered at the University of Malta and other educational institutions. The best approach depends on your learning style, your budget, and your level of commitment. It can be hard to fit learning into your life.

Language schools, such as Berlitz and inlingua, offer a range of Maltese courses, from beginner to advanced levels. They typically use a communicative approach, focusing on practical conversation skills and real-life situations. The classes are usually small, and the teachers are experienced in teaching Maltese to foreigners. It's a good option if you prefer a structured learning environment and want to interact with other learners. But it can be the more expensive option.

Private tutors can provide a more personalized learning experience, tailoring the lessons to your specific needs and goals. They can focus on your weaknesses, provide individual feedback, and adapt the pace of the lessons to your progress. It's a good option if you prefer one-on-one instruction and want to learn at your own pace. However, finding a good tutor can be challenging, and the cost can be higher than group classes.

Online resources and language learning apps, such as Duolingo, Memrise, and Babbel, offer a more flexible and affordable way to learn Maltese. They typically use a gamified approach, making learning fun and engaging. You can learn at your own pace, anytime, anywhere, and you can focus on the specific skills you want to develop, such as vocabulary, grammar, or pronunciation. However, they lack the personal interaction of a classroom or a tutor.

The University of Malta offers a range of Maltese language courses, from short introductory courses to full-degree programs. The courses are taught by experienced linguists and cover a wide range of topics, from Maltese grammar and literature to Maltese culture and history. It's a good option if you're interested in a more academic approach to learning Maltese, or if you're planning to pursue higher education in Malta. There is a vibrant academic scene in Malta.

Whatever approach you choose, it's important to be patient and persistent. Learning a new language takes time and effort, and Maltese is no exception. Don't be discouraged by the challenges, and don't be afraid to make mistakes. The Maltese are generally very forgiving of errors, and they appreciate the effort you're making to learn their language. The more you practice, the more confident you'll become.

One of the best ways to improve your Maltese is to immerse yourself in the language as much as possible. Watch Maltese TV shows and movies, listen to Maltese music, and read Maltese books and newspapers. Try to speak Maltese with your colleagues, your neighbors, and the shopkeepers you encounter in your daily life. Don't be shy; the Maltese are generally happy to help you practice your language skills.

You can also join a Maltese language exchange group or find a language partner online. This is a great way to practice your conversation skills and to learn from native speakers. You can meet people from all walks of life, learn about different aspects of Maltese culture, and make new friends. It's a fun and informal way to improve your language skills and to connect with the local community. It makes it a social activity too.

Another helpful tip is to learn some basic Maltese phrases before you arrive in Malta. This will help you navigate everyday situations, such as ordering food, asking for directions, and greeting people. Even a few simple phrases, such as "*bonġu*" (good morning), "*grazzi*" (thank you), and "*jekk jogħġbok*" (please), will go a long way. It shows that you're making an effort to learn the language, and it will be appreciated by the locals.

One of the challenges of learning Maltese is the lack of resources compared to more widely spoken languages. There are fewer textbooks, dictionaries, and online resources available, and it can be difficult to find authentic materials to practice with. However, the situation is improving, and there are more resources available now than ever before. You can find Maltese language books, CDs, and DVDs online and in some bookstores in Malta.

The Maltese language is constantly evolving, and new words and expressions are being added all the time. This is due to the influence of English, Italian, and other languages, as well as the creativity of the Maltese people themselves. The Maltese language is a living, breathing entity, and it reflects the changing culture and society of Malta. It's a fascinating language to study, and it offers a unique window into the Maltese soul.

One of the most rewarding aspects of learning Maltese is the ability to connect with the local culture on a deeper level. You'll be able to understand the nuances of Maltese humor, the subtleties of Maltese conversation, and the richness of Maltese literature and music. You'll also be able to participate more fully in Maltese social life, attending *festas*, joining local clubs, and making friends with Maltese people. It opens up a whole new world of experiences.

Learning Maltese is not just about acquiring a new skill; it's about embracing a new culture and a new way of life. It's about showing respect for the Maltese people and their heritage, and it's about demonstrating your commitment to becoming a part of the Maltese community. It's a challenging but ultimately rewarding journey, and it will enrich your expat experience in countless ways. So, *mela*, why not give it a try?

And now a few tips for learning some Maltese. Start with the basics: learn some common phrases and greetings. Focus on pronunciation: practice the unique sounds of Maltese. Don't be afraid to make mistakes: the Maltese are forgiving of errors. Immerse yourself in the language: watch Maltese TV, listen to Maltese music, read Maltese books. Practice speaking with native speakers: join a language exchange group or find a language partner.

Use online resources and language learning apps: Duolingo, Memrise, Babbel. Take classes at a language school or hire a private tutor. Consider taking a Maltese language course at the University of Malta. Be patient and persistent: learning a new language takes time and effort. And have fun! Learning Maltese should be an enjoyable experience. So, are you ready to give it a go?

One expression that will come in extremely useful in Malta is "*M'għandix idea*". This means "I have no idea", and if you master this phrase, and are able to say it like a native, you will hear it said a lot. You may well also find yourself saying it a lot too. This and "*Mela*" of course, which you will hear all of the time, everywhere you go.

There is a useful phrasebook and dictionary by Grazio Falzon, which contains many common words and phrases. This can be a very useful book to use. It has sections such as 'Greetings', 'Shopping', and 'At the Bank'. It also has sections about Maltese culture, tradition, and cuisine. It can be a good introduction to the Maltese language. And it will help you, if you are serious about it.

But, as has been said, you don't *need* to learn Maltese to get by in Malta. You can quite easily manage with English only. But learning the language can help. And it helps with integration, as well as helping you feel like part of Maltese society. It can be extremely rewarding. And the Maltese will greatly appreciate it. You might even get a discount.

CHAPTER TWELVE: Food, Glorious Food: Beyond *Pastizzi* (But Seriously, Eat the *Pastizzi*)

Right, let's get to the good stuff: the food. You've probably gathered by now that *pastizzi* are a Maltese obsession. They're cheap, they're delicious, and they're everywhere. But Maltese cuisine is so much more than just those flaky, cheesy (or pea-y) parcels of goodness. It's a vibrant, flavorful mix of Mediterranean, Arabic, Italian, and British influences, reflecting the island's rich and complex history. Prepare your taste buds for an adventure.

Think of Maltese food as a culinary tapestry, woven from centuries of trade, conquest, and cultural exchange. The base is Mediterranean, with an emphasis on fresh, seasonal ingredients like tomatoes, olives, capers, and garlic. Then you have the Arabic influence, adding spices like cumin, coriander, and cinnamon. The Italian touch brings pasta, pizza, and a love of hearty, rustic dishes. And the British, well, they left behind a fondness for pies, pasties, and a good cup of tea.

The result is a cuisine that's both familiar and exotic, comforting and exciting. It's a cuisine that celebrates simple, honest flavors, and it's meant to be shared with family and friends. Meals are often long, leisurely affairs, with multiple courses and plenty of wine. The Maltese love to eat, and they love to feed others. Don't be surprised if you're offered second helpings, even if you're already bursting at the seams.

Let's start with the *pastizzi*, since we can't seem to stop talking about them. These are the quintessential Maltese snack, and you'll find them in *pastizzerias* (pastizzi shops) on almost every street corner. They're made with a flaky, phyllo-like pastry and filled with either ricotta cheese (*pastizzi tal-irkotta*) or mushy peas (*pastizzi tal-piżelli*). They're best eaten hot, straight from the oven, and they're incredibly addictive. Don't say we didn't warn you.

But *pastizzi* are just the beginning. There's a whole world of Maltese snacks and street food to explore. *Ftira*, a type of Maltese bread, is another staple. It's often filled with a mixture of tuna, tomatoes, olives, capers, and onions, making a delicious and satisfying lunch. *Ħobż biż-żejt* is another simple but delicious snack, consisting of crusty Maltese bread rubbed with tomato paste, drizzled with olive oil, and sprinkled with salt and pepper.

For something a bit more substantial, try *timpana*, a baked pasta dish that's similar to a lasagna, but with a richer, more savory flavor. It's made with layers of pasta, meat sauce, hard-boiled eggs, and cheese, all encased in a pastry crust. It's a hearty, comforting dish that's perfect for a cold winter evening. Or any evening, really. It's another favorite with the Maltese. And it can be quite heavy.

Fenek (rabbit stew) is often considered the national dish of Malta. It's a slow-cooked stew, typically made with rabbit, red wine, tomatoes, onions, garlic, and herbs. The rabbit is tender and flavorful, and the sauce is rich and aromatic. It's traditionally served with potatoes or pasta, and it's a dish that's meant to be savored. It's a true taste of Malta, and it's a must-try for any visitor.

Lampuki (dorado or mahi-mahi) is a type of fish that's popular in Malta, especially during the autumn months. It's often served grilled, fried, or baked, and it's a delicious and healthy option. *Lampuki pie* is another traditional dish, made with lampuki, vegetables, and a flaky pastry crust. It's a savory and satisfying pie that's perfect for a light lunch or dinner. This is often very popular indeed.

Seafood is, unsurprisingly, a major part of the Maltese diet. You'll find a wide variety of fresh fish and shellfish available in restaurants and markets. *Aljotta* is a traditional Maltese fish soup, made with fish, tomatoes, garlic, rice, and herbs. It's a light and flavorful soup that's perfect for a starter or a light meal. *Stuffat tal-qarnit* (octopus stew) is another popular seafood dish, slow-cooked with tomatoes, onions, garlic, and olives.

Maltese cuisine also features a variety of vegetable dishes, often reflecting the seasonal produce available. *Kapunata* is a Maltese version of ratatouille, made with eggplant, tomatoes, peppers, onions, capers, and olives. It's a flavorful and versatile dish that can be served hot or cold, as a side dish or a main course. *Qarabagħli mimli* (stuffed zucchini) is another popular vegetable dish, often filled with a mixture of rice, meat, and herbs.

For those with a sweet tooth, Maltese desserts offer a delightful range of flavors and textures. *Imqaret* are deep-fried date pastries, often served with a scoop of vanilla ice cream. They're crispy on the outside, soft and sweet on the inside, and utterly irresistible. *Kannoli* are similar to Italian cannoli, consisting of crispy pastry tubes filled with sweet ricotta cheese. They're a popular treat, especially during *festas* and other celebrations.

Helwa tat-Tork is a sweet, dense confection made with sesame seeds, sugar, and almonds. It's similar to Turkish delight, and it's often served with coffee or tea. *Kwareżimal* are traditional Lenten biscuits, made with almonds, honey, and spices. They're a bit like biscotti, and they're perfect for dunking in coffee or tea. They're a seasonal treat, but they're worth seeking out if you're in Malta during Lent.

Maltese cuisine also features a variety of breads and pastries. The traditional Maltese loaf is a crusty, sourdough bread with a soft, airy interior. It's perfect for soaking up sauces or enjoying with a simple spread of butter or olive oil. *Ftira*, as mentioned earlier, is another type of Maltese bread, often used for sandwiches. It's a flatter, denser bread than the traditional loaf, and it has a slightly chewy texture.

When it comes to drinks, Malta offers a range of local and imported options. *Kinnie* is a unique Maltese soft drink, made with bitter oranges and aromatic herbs. It has a distinctive bittersweet flavor that's not for everyone, but it's worth trying at least once. It's often described as an acquired taste, but many people find it incredibly refreshing, especially on a hot day. You will either love it, or hate it.

Cisk is the most popular local beer, a light and refreshing lager that's perfect for the Maltese climate. There are also a number of other local beers, including Hopleaf Pale Ale and Blue Label Ale. Maltese wines are also gaining in popularity, with several wineries producing a range of red, white, and rosé wines. The local grape varieties, Gellewza and Ghirghentina, produce unique and flavorful wines.

If you're looking for something stronger, try a glass of *bajtra*, a liqueur made from prickly pears. It's a sweet and fruity liqueur that's often served as a *digestivo* after a meal. There are also a number of local liqueurs made with herbs, spices, and fruits, such as aniseed, carob, and honey. They're often homemade, and they're a great way to experience the traditional flavors of Malta.

Eating out in Malta is a popular pastime, and there are restaurants and cafes to suit every taste and budget. From Michelin-starred restaurants to humble *pastizzerias*, you'll find a wide range of dining options. The Maltese love to socialize over food and drink, and meals can be long, leisurely affairs. Don't be surprised if you're offered a complimentary *digestivo* after your meal; it's a Maltese tradition.

If you're on a budget, there are plenty of affordable options for eating out in Malta. *Pastizzerias, ftira* shops, and small cafes offer inexpensive snacks and meals. You can also find numerous restaurants serving pizzas, pastas, and other simple dishes at reasonable prices. If you're willing to venture beyond the tourist hotspots, you'll find even more affordable options, often with a more authentic Maltese flavor.

For a more upscale dining experience, there are several fine-dining restaurants in Malta, particularly in Valletta and St. Julian's. These restaurants often feature innovative cuisine, using fresh, local ingredients and creative culinary techniques. Some of them have even earned Michelin stars, recognizing their exceptional quality and service. However, be prepared to pay a premium for this level of dining. It will be a memorable experience.

One of the best ways to experience Maltese cuisine is to visit the local markets. The Marsaxlokk fish market, held every Sunday, is a must-see for seafood lovers. You'll find a wide variety of fresh fish and shellfish, caught by local fishermen. It's a vibrant and colorful market, and it's a great place to experience the local culture. You can also buy fresh produce, local cheeses, and other Maltese specialties.

The Valletta market, held daily, is another great place to find fresh produce, local products, and souvenirs. It's a bustling market, with vendors selling everything from fruits and vegetables to clothes and household goods. It's a great place to soak up the atmosphere and to practice your haggling skills. Just remember to be polite and respectful, and don't expect to get a huge discount.

If you're interested in learning more about Maltese cuisine, you can take a cooking class or a food tour. Several companies offer cooking classes where you can learn to prepare traditional Maltese dishes, such as *pastizzi*, *fenek*, and *timpana*. Food tours are another great way to explore the local culinary scene, visiting markets, restaurants, and food producers. You'll learn about the history and traditions of Maltese food, and you'll get to sample a variety of delicious dishes.

Maltese cuisine is a reflection of the island's rich and diverse culture. It's a blend of Mediterranean, Arabic, Italian, and British influences, creating a unique and flavorful culinary experience. From the humble *pastizz* to the elaborate *festa* feasts, Maltese food is all about sharing, celebrating, and enjoying the simple pleasures of life. So, embrace the culinary adventure, try new things, and don't be afraid to ask for recommendations.

And, of course, eat the *pastizzi*. Seriously, eat them. Eat all of them. You won't regret it. But your waistline might. Just remember to balance your *pastizzi* consumption with some fresh fruit and vegetables, and maybe a walk along the coast. It's all about moderation, even in Malta. Although, given the Maltese love of food, moderation can be a bit of a challenge. But that is all part of the fun.

One thing you may well find is that you will put on weight during your first few weeks and months in Malta. This is not unusual. It is largely a result of the different food, and the change of lifestyle. So if this does happen to you, do not worry too much. It is quite common. And you can always try to eat healthier, after a while.

But for now, enjoy all the food that Malta has to offer. It really is a melting pot of different cuisines. And there is something to appeal to all tastes. It is very unlikely that you will struggle to find things you like. And you will soon get used to the food, and discover your own favorites. You may well find yourself buying recipe books.

So explore, experiment, and try new things. Ask the Maltese people for their recommendations. They will be more than happy to tell you their favorite dishes, and where to eat them. And be prepared to put on a little weight. But do not worry - it is worth it. Food is a very important part of Maltese culture. And it will be a very important part of your Maltese adventure.

CHAPTER THIRTEEN: Leisure and Entertainment: Sun, Sea, and Siestas (The Holy Trinity)

Right, you've unpacked your boxes, wrestled with the bureaucracy, and maybe even learned to say "bongu" without sounding like you're gargling seawater. Now it's time for the *real* reason you moved to Malta: the leisure and entertainment. Forget the tax breaks and the career opportunities; we all know you're here for the sun, the sea, and the gloriously lazy afternoons. And, *mela*, Malta delivers. In spades, buckets, and overflowing *pastizzi* platters.

Think of Maltese leisure as a three-legged stool. One leg is the sun, that glorious, relentless Mediterranean sun that beats down on the island for most of the year. The second leg is the sea, the crystal-clear, turquoise waters that surround Malta, Gozo, and Comino. And the third leg is the siesta, that sacred afternoon nap that allows you to recharge your batteries and prepare for another round of sun and sea. It's a simple formula, but it works.

Let's start with the sun. Malta boasts over 300 days of sunshine per year, making it one of the sunniest countries in Europe. The summers are hot and dry, with temperatures often reaching 30°C (86°F) or higher. The winters are mild, with temperatures rarely dropping below 10°C (50°F). This means that you can enjoy outdoor activities year-round, from swimming and sunbathing to hiking and exploring. Just remember to pack your sunscreen. Seriously, pack *lots* of sunscreen.

The sun is not just a source of warmth and light; it's a way of life in Malta. It dictates the rhythm of the day, from the early morning swims to the late-night gatherings on the beach. It's the reason why the Maltese are so relaxed and laid-back, and it's the reason why you'll find yourself spending most of your time outdoors. Embrace the sun, but respect its power. Sunburns are not a good look, and heatstroke is even worse.

Now, let's talk about the sea. Malta is surrounded by some of the clearest, cleanest waters in the Mediterranean. The sea is a playground for swimmers, snorkelers, divers, and boaters. There are numerous beaches to choose from, from the sandy stretches of Mellieha Bay and Golden Bay to the rocky coves of St. Peter's Pool and Ghar Lapsi. Each beach has its own unique charm, and you'll find yourself exploring them all. It will take time.

Swimming is a national pastime in Malta, and you'll find people of all ages taking a dip in the sea, from toddlers splashing in the shallows to elderly men doing their daily laps. The water is generally calm and safe, but it's always a good idea to check the conditions before you swim. There can be strong currents in some areas, and jellyfish are occasionally present. Look out for warning flags on the beaches, and don't swim alone if you're not a strong swimmer.

Snorkeling and diving are also popular activities in Malta. The clear waters and abundant marine life make it a paradise for underwater explorers. There are numerous dive sites around the islands, from shallow reefs teeming with colorful fish to deep wrecks that attract experienced divers. You can rent equipment from dive shops and join guided tours, or you can explore on your own if you're a certified diver. Just remember to follow safe diving practices.

Boating is another popular way to enjoy the Maltese sea. You can rent a small boat and explore the coastline at your own pace, or you can join a boat trip to Comino and the Blue Lagoon. There are also several companies offering sailing charters, allowing you to experience the thrill of sailing in the Mediterranean. If you're feeling adventurous, you can even try your hand at windsurfing, kitesurfing, or jet skiing. The possibilities are endless.

And now, the third leg of the stool: the siesta. The siesta is a traditional afternoon break, typically taken between 1 pm and 4 pm, during the hottest part of the day. It's a time to relax, recharge, and escape the heat. Many shops and businesses close during the siesta, and the streets become quiet. It's a cultural institution, and it's a great way to adapt to the Maltese pace of life. Embrace the siesta.

The siesta is not just about sleeping, although that's certainly a popular option. It's about taking a break from the hustle and bustle of the day and enjoying a moment of peace and tranquility. You can read a book, listen to music, or simply sit on your balcony and enjoy the view. It's a time to slow down, relax, and appreciate the simple pleasures of life. It's a Maltese tradition, and it's one you'll quickly learn to love.

Beyond the holy trinity of sun, sea, and siestas, Malta offers a wide range of other leisure and entertainment options. There are numerous historical sites to explore, from the Neolithic temples of Hagar Qim and Mnajdra to the medieval city of Mdina and the Baroque capital of Valletta. Each site tells a story of Malta's rich and complex history, and they're a must-see for any visitor. Take your time and do some research.

Valletta, a UNESCO World Heritage site, is a treasure trove of historical and cultural attractions. You can visit St. John's Co-Cathedral, a masterpiece of Baroque architecture, or explore the Grand Master's Palace, the former residence of the Knights of St. John. The city is also home to numerous museums, art galleries, and theaters, offering a vibrant cultural scene. It's a city that rewards exploration, and you'll find something new every time you visit.

Mdina, the "Silent City," is another must-see destination. It's a medieval walled city perched on a hilltop, offering breathtaking views of the surrounding countryside. Stepping into Mdina is like stepping back in time, and it's easy to imagine knights in shining armor clanking down the cobblestone streets. It's a place of tranquility and beauty, and it's a perfect escape from the hustle and bustle of modern life.

The Three Cities, Vittoriosa, Senglea, and Cospicua, are another historical gem. They're located across the Grand Harbour from Valletta, and they offer a glimpse into Malta's maritime past. You can explore the fortifications, visit the Inquisitor's Palace, and wander through the narrow, winding streets. It's a less touristy area than Valletta or Mdina, and it offers a more authentic glimpse of Maltese life.

For those who enjoy the outdoors, Malta offers numerous hiking and walking trails. The coastline is particularly scenic, with dramatic cliffs, hidden coves, and stunning views. You can hike along the Dingli Cliffs, the highest point on the island, or explore the rugged beauty of the north coast. There are also several nature reserves and parks, offering opportunities for birdwatching, wildlife spotting, and simply enjoying the natural beauty of the Maltese islands.

If you're a fan of nightlife, Malta has plenty to offer. Paceville, in St. Julian's, is the main entertainment district, with numerous bars, clubs, and restaurants. It's a lively and energetic area, especially during the summer months, and it attracts a young, international crowd. If you're looking for a more relaxed atmosphere, there are plenty of other options, from wine bars and jazz clubs to traditional Maltese pubs.

Malta also hosts a number of festivals and events throughout the year. The village *festas*, mentioned earlier, are a highlight of the Maltese calendar, with fireworks, processions, and plenty of food and drink. There are also numerous cultural events, such as the Malta Arts Festival, the Malta Jazz Festival, and the Notte Bianca, a night-time celebration of arts and culture. Carnival, held in February, is another major event, with colorful parades, elaborate costumes, and a general atmosphere of revelry.

If you're a sports enthusiast, Malta offers a range of options. Football is the most popular sport, and the Maltese are passionate about their local teams. You can attend a match at the National Stadium in Ta' Qali, or catch a game at one of the smaller stadiums around the island. Water sports, as mentioned earlier, are also popular, and there are opportunities for swimming, diving, sailing, and windsurfing. There are also several golf courses, tennis courts, and gyms.

For those who enjoy shopping, Malta offers a mix of local and international brands. Sliema and Valletta are the main shopping destinations, with a range of department stores, boutiques, and souvenir shops. There are also several shopping malls, such as The Point in Sliema and Bay Street in St. Julian's, offering a more modern shopping experience. If you're looking for local products, visit the markets in Valletta and Marsaxlokk, where you can find fresh produce, crafts, and souvenirs.

If you're traveling with children, Malta offers a range of family-friendly activities. There are several beaches with shallow waters and sandy shores, perfect for young children. There are also several water parks, such as Splash & Fun and Popeye Village, offering a fun day out for the whole family. The Malta National Aquarium is another popular attraction, with a variety of marine life on display.

Malta's small size makes it easy to explore, and you can easily combine different activities in a single day. You can start with a swim in the morning, followed by a visit to a historical site in the afternoon, and finish with a delicious meal at a local restaurant in the evening. Or you can simply spend the day relaxing on the beach, soaking up the sun, and enjoying the siesta. The choice is yours.

One of the best things about Malta is that it offers something for everyone. Whether you're a history buff, a beach lover, a foodie, a nightlife enthusiast, or a sports fan, you'll find plenty to keep you entertained. And with its warm climate, friendly people, and relaxed pace of life, Malta is a great place to unwind, recharge, and enjoy the simple pleasures of life. Just don't forget the sunscreen.

Malta also has a thriving arts and culture scene. There are numerous art galleries showcasing the work of local and international artists. The Manoel Theatre in Valletta is one of the oldest working theaters in Europe and hosts a variety of performances, including plays, operas, and concerts. There are also several smaller theaters and performance spaces around the island, offering a diverse range of entertainment.

For music lovers, Malta offers a variety of options, from classical concerts and opera performances to jazz clubs and rock bars. The Malta Jazz Festival, held every July, is a major event, attracting international artists and jazz enthusiasts from around the world. There are also numerous local bands and musicians performing in bars and clubs throughout the island. You'll find a vibrant and diverse music scene in Malta.

Cinema is also popular in Malta, and there are several multiplex cinemas showing the latest international releases. The Eden Cinemas in St. Julian's is the largest cinema complex, with multiple screens and a variety of food and drink options. There are also smaller, independent cinemas, such as the Embassy Cinema in Valletta, offering a more intimate viewing experience. You can catch the latest Hollywood blockbusters or enjoy an art-house film.

If you're looking for something a bit different, you can try your luck at one of Malta's casinos. The Dragonara Casino in St. Julian's is the largest and most famous, housed in a stunning 19th-century palace. There are also several smaller casinos, offering a range of games, from slot machines and poker to blackjack and roulette. Gambling is legal in Malta, and the casinos are regulated by the Malta Gaming Authority.

For those who enjoy a bit of pampering, Malta offers a range of spas and wellness centers. You can indulge in a massage, a facial, or a body treatment, or simply relax in a sauna or a jacuzzi. Many hotels have their own spas, and there are also several independent spas offering a variety of treatments. It's a great way to unwind and de-stress after a busy day of exploring or working.

CHAPTER FOURTEEN: Making Friends: From Expats to Locals (and Avoiding the Awkward "Where Are You *Really* From?" Question)

So, you've landed in Malta, navigated the initial hurdles, and you're starting to settle in. Now comes the next challenge: making friends. Unless you're a hermit who thrives on solitude and conversations with *pastizzi* (no judgment), you're going to want some human interaction. But where do you start? How do you connect with people in a new country, with a different culture, and a language that sounds like a cat coughing up a fur ball?

Think of making friends in Malta as a two-pronged approach. On one side, you have the expat community: a diverse group of people from all over the world who, like you, have chosen to make Malta their home. On the other side, you have the locals: the Maltese people themselves, with their unique culture, traditions, and, *mela*, their own way of doing things. Both groups offer opportunities for friendship, but they require slightly different approaches.

Let's start with the expats. Malta attracts people from all walks of life, from digital nomads and retirees to iGaming employees and finance professionals. You'll find expats from the UK, Scandinavia, Germany, France, Italy, the US, Australia, and pretty much every other corner of the globe. They're all in the same boat as you, navigating a new country and looking for connections. This shared experience creates a natural bond, and it's relatively easy to strike up conversations.

There are numerous ways to connect with other expats in Malta. Online forums and Facebook groups are a great starting point. You'll find groups dedicated to expats in Malta, expats from specific countries, expats with specific interests (hiking, diving, book clubs, etc.), and even expats who just want to complain about the Maltese bureaucracy (a popular pastime, believe us). These groups are a valuable source of information, support, and social events.

Another way to meet expats is to attend events and activities specifically targeted at the international community. There are regular meetups, pub quizzes, language exchanges, and networking events organized by various groups and organizations. These events are a great way to meet people in a relaxed and informal setting, and you're likely to find someone who shares your interests or background. Just be prepared for the inevitable "Where are you from?" question.

Co-working spaces, mentioned earlier, are also a great place to meet other expats, especially if you're working remotely or freelancing. These spaces offer a sense of community and a chance to interact with people who are in a similar situation to you. You can share experiences, exchange tips, and maybe even collaborate on projects. It's a more productive way to make friends than hanging around in bars, although that's also an option.

If you're into sports or hobbies, joining a local club or group is another way to meet expats and locals alike. There are clubs for everything from football and rugby to sailing and hiking. It's a great way to stay active, pursue your interests, and meet people who share your passions. And, who knows, you might even discover a new hobby you never knew you had. Maltese pastimes are many and varied.

One of the advantages of befriending other expats is that they understand the challenges and frustrations of adjusting to life in a new country. They can offer advice, support, and a sympathetic ear when you're feeling homesick or overwhelmed. They can also share their experiences of navigating the Maltese system, from finding a doctor to dealing with the dreaded Identity Malta. It's a valuable support network, and it can make the transition to life in Malta much easier.

However, it's also important to connect with the local Maltese community. This is where you'll truly experience the Maltese culture and gain a deeper understanding of the island and its people. Making friends with locals can be a bit more challenging than befriending expats, as the Maltese tend to be quite close-knit and family-oriented. But it's definitely worth the effort, and it will enrich your expat experience immeasurably. And it will repay the effort you make.

One of the best ways to meet locals is through work or school. If you're working in Malta, your colleagues are a natural starting point for building relationships. Invite them for a coffee or a drink after work, or join them for a company event. If you have children in school, get involved in the school community and meet other parents. These connections can lead to friendships and a deeper integration into Maltese life.

Another way to meet locals is to get involved in your local community. Attend village *festas*, join a local sports club, or volunteer for a local charity. These activities will give you a chance to interact with Maltese people in a natural and informal setting, and you'll likely find that they're welcoming and friendly. Just be prepared for a lot of noise, a lot of food, and a lot of passionate conversations.

Learning some Maltese, as discussed earlier, is another great way to connect with the locals. Even a few basic phrases will be greatly appreciated, and it shows that you're making an effort to understand and appreciate their culture. The Maltese are generally very forgiving of language errors, and they'll be happy to help you practice your Maltese. It's a great conversation starter, and it can lead to some interesting and amusing interactions.

One thing to be aware of is that the Maltese sense of humor can be quite dry and sarcastic. They love to tease each other, and they're not afraid to make fun of themselves or their situations. Don't be offended if a Maltese person makes a joke at your expense; it's usually meant in good humor. Just be prepared to give as good as you get, and don't take yourself too seriously. It is all part of the fun.

Another thing to be aware of is the Maltese concept of "*pika*," the rivalry or competition that exists between different villages, football teams, and even political parties. It's a complex concept, and it can be both a source of amusement and a cause of conflict. It's best to avoid getting involved in heated discussions about *pika*, especially if you're not familiar with the nuances of the situation. Just observe, listen, and learn.

Making friends with locals takes time and effort, but it's worth it. You'll gain a deeper understanding of Maltese culture, you'll learn about the local traditions and customs, and you'll discover hidden gems that you wouldn't find in any guidebook. You'll also experience the warmth and hospitality of the Maltese people, and you'll feel like you truly belong in your new home. It's a rewarding experience, and it will make your time in Malta much richer.

One of the challenges of making friends in Malta, whether with expats or locals, can be the transient nature of the expat community. People come and go, and friendships can be fleeting. It's important to be prepared for this, and to cherish the connections you make, even if they're only for a short time. It's also important to be open to making new friends constantly, as people move on and new people arrive.

Another challenge can be the cultural differences. The Maltese way of life is different from what you might be used to, and it can take time to adjust. Be patient, be open-minded, and be willing to learn. Don't try to impose your own cultural norms on others, and be respectful of the Maltese way of doing things. It's all about finding a balance between adapting to a new culture and staying true to yourself.

Making friends in Malta is a journey, not a destination. It takes time, effort, and a willingness to step outside your comfort zone. But it's also one of the most rewarding aspects of the expat experience. You'll meet people from all walks of life, you'll learn about different cultures, and you'll form connections that will last a lifetime. So, embrace the challenge, be open to new experiences, and don't be afraid to put yourself out there.

And now for a few friendship tips, to help you navigate the social scene in Malta. Join online forums and Facebook groups for expats. Attend events and activities targeted at the international community. Join a local sports club or hobby group. Get involved in your local community. Learn some basic Maltese phrases. Be open to meeting people from different backgrounds and cultures.

Be patient and persistent: making friends takes time. Don't be afraid to initiate conversations and invite people for coffee or drinks. Be respectful of Maltese culture and traditions. Don't take yourself too seriously, and be prepared to laugh at yourself. Be prepared for the transient nature of the expat community. And cherish the connections you make, even if they're only for a short time. And don't be discouraged.

One of the best ways to make friends is to be a good listener. People appreciate it when you take an interest in their lives and listen to their stories. Ask questions, show empathy, and be genuinely interested in what they have to say. It's a simple but effective way to build rapport and form connections. And it's a skill that will serve you well in all areas of your life, not just in making friends.

Another important tip is to be yourself. Don't try to be someone you're not, or pretend to be interested in things you're not. Authenticity is key to forming genuine connections. People can spot a fake a mile away, and they're much more likely to be drawn to someone who is genuine and comfortable in their own skin. So, be yourself, embrace your quirks, and let your personality shine through.

Don't be afraid to ask for help or advice. People are generally happy to help, and it's a great way to start a conversation and build a connection. Whether you're asking for directions, recommendations for a good restaurant, or advice on navigating the Maltese bureaucracy, asking for help shows that you're open to learning and that you value other people's opinions. It's a simple but effective way to break the ice.

Be open to new experiences. Malta offers a wide range of activities and events, from *festas* and cultural performances to hiking and water sports. Try new things, step outside your comfort zone, and be open to exploring all that Malta has to offer. You'll meet new people, discover new interests, and create lasting memories. And you'll probably have some hilarious stories to tell along the way.

Don't be discouraged if you don't make friends immediately. It takes time to build relationships, and it's normal to feel a bit lonely or isolated at first. Be patient, be persistent, and keep putting yourself out there. The more you interact with people, the more likely you are to form connections. And remember, everyone is in the same boat, especially in the expat community.

Making friends in Malta is an essential part of the expat experience. It's a way to build a support network, to learn about a new culture, and to feel like you belong in your new home. It's a journey that requires effort, patience, and a willingness to step outside your comfort zone. But it's also a journey that's filled with opportunities for connection, growth, and unforgettable experiences. So, go out there, meet people, and start building your Maltese social circle.

One final thing that is worth being aware of is the "small island" mentality. As Malta is a small island (as has been frequently mentioned), news and gossip travel quickly. Everyone seems to know everyone. And everyone seems to know everyone's business. You will quickly realize this. And you will quickly realize that your own business becomes part of this. It is not meant in a nasty way, normally. But it is something to be aware of.

And it is something to be careful about. Because anything you do or say is likely to become public knowledge, very quickly. This "small island" mentality is part of Malta. It is not something you will be able to change. So you just have to be aware of it, and not let it worry you. It is just part of the experience of making friends, and building a social circle.

So go out there and socialize. Meet people. And don't be afraid to ask for help. Befriend locals. And befriend fellow expats. Malta is a great place to make friends. And having a social circle will make your stay more enjoyable. And make you adjust to your life in Malta. So take advantage of the opportunities.

And don't worry too much about the "where are you *really* from?" question. This question is often asked, especially by the Maltese. It is not meant to be offensive. It is just their way of finding out more about you. And a way of finding a connection. So don't be offended by it. Just answer honestly. It is all part of making friends.

Making friends is an important part of life anywhere. And when you are in a new country, it can make your time there a better experience. Having a social circle makes your time in a place more satisfying. And nowhere is this more so than in Malta. So make the most of the opportunities here, and you will find Malta a welcoming place. And you will settle in more easily.

Making friends in Malta is not hard. The Maltese are friendly. And there is a large expat community. It is there to be taken advantage of. So get out there, meet people and make friends. And avoid that awkward "Where are you *really* from?" question. And before long you will have built a new and fulfilling life in Malta.

CHAPTER FIFTEEN: Dealing with Bureaucracy: The Maltese National Sport (After Football)

Alright, brace yourselves. We're about to delve into the murky, often maddening, world of Maltese bureaucracy. If you thought navigating the visa process was a challenge, you ain't seen nothing yet. Dealing with officialdom in Malta is an experience, a rite of passage, and a test of your patience, resilience, and sense of humor. Think of it as a national sport, like football, but with more paperwork, longer queues, and a higher chance of wanting to tear your hair out.

The Maltese bureaucracy is a complex beast, a multi-headed hydra of government departments, local councils, and regulatory bodies. It's a system that seems to operate on its own unique logic, where the rules are often unclear, the processes are unnecessarily complicated, and the outcome is frequently unpredictable. It's a world of forms, stamps, signatures, and endless waiting, where the simplest task can turn into a multi-day, multi-office odyssey. You will *not* like it.

Why is Maltese bureaucracy so… *special*? There are several contributing factors. One is the island's history. Centuries of colonial rule, with different powers imposing their own administrative systems, have created a layered and often contradictory bureaucratic structure. Another factor is the small size of the country. Everyone knows everyone, and personal connections can often play a role in how things get done (or don't get done). This can be frustrating.

Another factor is the Maltese culture, which, as we've discussed, has a relaxed approach to time and a fondness for rules and regulations. This combination can lead to a situation where things move slowly, and there's a lot of red tape to cut through. It's not that the Maltese are deliberately trying to be difficult; it's just that the system has evolved this way, and it's deeply ingrained in the way things are done.

So, how do you deal with Maltese bureaucracy? The first rule is: be prepared. Gather all your documents, make copies of everything, and keep them organized. You'll likely need your passport, your residence permit, your ID card, proof of address, and a whole host of other documents, depending on what you're trying to achieve. The more prepared you are, the less likely you are to encounter delays and frustration.

The second rule is: be patient. Things take time in Malta, and there's no point in getting agitated or losing your temper. It won't speed things up, and it might even make things worse. Accept that you're going to have to wait, that you'll probably have to visit multiple offices, and that you might have to fill out the same form several times. It's all part of the process.

The third rule is: be polite and respectful. Even if you're frustrated, even if you think the system is ridiculous, always be polite to the people you're dealing with. They're just doing their job, and they're probably just as frustrated with the system as you are. Losing your temper won't help, and it might even make them less likely to assist you. A smile and a "please" and "thank you" can go a long way.

The fourth rule is: learn some basic Maltese phrases. While most government officials speak English, knowing a few Maltese phrases will be greatly appreciated. It shows that you're making an effort to understand and appreciate their culture, and it can help to build rapport. Even a simple "*bonġu*" (good morning) or "*grazzi*" (thank you) can make a difference. It's a sign of respect, and it might even get you a slightly faster service.

The fifth rule is: don't be afraid to ask for help. If you're struggling to understand a form, or if you're not sure what to do next, ask for clarification. The officials are usually happy to explain things, although they might not always be able to do it in perfect English. If you're really stuck, consider hiring a translator or a consultant who specializes in navigating Maltese bureaucracy. It might cost you money, but save your sanity.

One of the most common bureaucratic hurdles you'll encounter is dealing with Identity Malta, the agency responsible for residency permits, ID cards, and other identity-related matters. As discussed in Chapter Two, the process of obtaining a residency permit can be lengthy and complicated. But even after you've got your permit, you'll likely have to deal with Identity Malta again for renewals, updates, and other administrative tasks. Be prepared for long queues and lots of paperwork.

Another common challenge is dealing with local councils. These are responsible for a wide range of local services, from waste collection and street cleaning to building permits and parking regulations. Each council has its own set of rules and procedures, and they can vary significantly from one locality to another. If you need to apply for a permit, report a problem, or simply find out information, you'll need to contact your local council.

The process of obtaining a building permit, for example, can be notoriously complex and time-consuming. You'll need to submit detailed plans, pay fees, and obtain approvals from various departments. The process can take months, or even years, and there's no guarantee that your application will be approved. If you're planning any major renovations or construction work, it's advisable to hire an architect or a consultant who is familiar with the local regulations.

Dealing with utility companies can also be a bureaucratic challenge. Setting up electricity, water, and internet services can involve multiple phone calls, emails, and visits to different offices. You'll need to provide proof of address, your ID card, and possibly other documents. The process can be slow and frustrating, especially if you're dealing with multiple providers. Be persistent, keep track of your communications, and don't be afraid to escalate your complaint if necessary.

Opening a bank account, as discussed in Chapter Four, can also involve a significant amount of bureaucracy. You'll need to provide your passport, your residence permit, proof of address, and possibly other documents. The bank might also ask you to provide a reference letter from your previous bank, proof of income, and a detailed explanation of your financial history. The process can take several weeks, and you might need to attend an in-person interview at a branch.

Even seemingly simple tasks, such as registering a car or obtaining a parking permit, can involve a surprising amount of paperwork and bureaucracy. You'll need to fill out forms, provide documents, and pay fees. The process can be confusing, and the rules can vary depending on your circumstances. It's always a good idea to check the requirements in advance and to gather all the necessary documents before you start.

One of the quirks of Maltese bureaucracy is the prevalence of stamps. You'll encounter stamps on all sorts of documents, from official forms to receipts. The stamps are often used to indicate that a fee has been paid or that a document has been processed. Don't be surprised if you're asked to provide a stamped copy of a document, even if you've already submitted the original. It's just the way things are done.

Another quirk is the importance of personal connections. As mentioned earlier, Malta is a small country, and everyone seems to know everyone. This means that personal relationships can often play a role in how things get done. If you know someone who works in a particular government department or local council, they might be able to help you navigate the system or speed up a process. It's not always fair, but it's a reality of life in Malta.

Despite the challenges, it's important to remember that the Maltese bureaucracy is not insurmountable. With patience, persistence, and a good sense of humor, you can navigate the system and get things done. Don't be afraid to ask for help, and don't be discouraged by setbacks. It's all part of the Maltese experience, and it will give you a deeper understanding of the island and its culture.

One of the best ways to deal with Maltese bureaucracy is to develop a network of contacts. Get to know your neighbors, your colleagues, and other expats. They might be able to offer advice, share their experiences, or even introduce you to someone who can help you with a particular issue. Building relationships is key to navigating the system, and it can make the process much less stressful.

Another helpful tip is to keep a detailed record of all your communications with government departments, local councils, and other organizations. Note down the dates, times, names of people you spoke to, and any relevant reference numbers. This will help you keep track of your progress, and it can be useful if you need to follow up on a request or make a complaint. It's also a good idea to keep copies of all the documents you submit.

If you're dealing with a particularly complex or frustrating issue, consider hiring a professional to help you. There are lawyers, accountants, and consultants who specialize in navigating Maltese bureaucracy. They can provide advice, represent you in dealings with government departments, and generally make the process much smoother. It's an additional expense, but it can save you a lot of time, stress, and potential mistakes.

One of the most important things to remember is to stay calm and positive. Getting angry or frustrated won't help, and it might even make things worse. Take a deep breath, remind yourself that it's all part of the Maltese experience, and try to find the humor in the situation. You'll probably have some hilarious stories to tell your friends and family back home.

Maltese bureaucracy is a challenge, but it's also an opportunity to learn about the Maltese culture and to develop your patience and resilience. It's a test of your adaptability and your ability to navigate a complex system. And, ultimately, it's a rewarding experience that will make you appreciate the simple things in life, like a functioning internet connection or a parking permit that doesn't require a PhD in Maltese law.

And now for a few specific situations where you might encounter bureaucracy. If you are registering a birth, you need to go to the Public Registry, with the relevant documents. There may be a queue. If you are registering a marriage, you again need to go to the Public Registry, with the relevant documents, and various forms. There may be a queue.

If you are applying for citizenship, this is more complicated. You need to contact the Citizenship Unit, and fill in a lot of forms. And provide a lot of documents. And there will almost certainly be a queue. And a long wait. For all of these things, you need to be prepared for a wait.

If you are registering a death... well, you won't be doing that yourself, obviously. But someone will need to do it, at the Public Registry, with various forms and documents. And there may be a queue. So you can see that there is a common theme.

If you are registering a company, the relevant place is the Malta Business Registry. There will be forms, documents, and fees. If you are dealing with a planning application, the relevant place is the Planning Authority. There will be forms, documents, and fees. If you are dealing with a tax matter, the relevant place is the Inland Revenue Department. There will be forms, documents, and quite possibly, a long wait.

So dealing with Maltese bureaucracy can often feel like an uphill struggle. It can involve a lot of different procedures, a lot of forms, and often a lot of waiting. But it can be done, and it is a necessary part of living in Malta. So take a deep breath, and be prepared.

The Maltese themselves have to deal with all of these things as well. It is not just something that is reserved for expats. So do not feel that you are being singled out in any way. It can feel like it sometimes, but that is not the case. Everyone has to do it.

And once it's done, it's done. You will not have to go through it again, at least, not for a while. Until the next time. Which may be sooner than you think. But that is all part of the fun of dealing with Maltese bureaucracy. Embrace it.

So you can see that there is a common theme in all of these situations. There will be forms. There will be documents. There will be fees. And there will be waiting. This is the essence of Maltese bureaucracy. Learn it. And get used to it. You will have to, if you are going to live in Malta.

Dealing with bureaucracy is part of life in most countries, and Malta is no exception. But in Malta, it can be a little different. It is more ingrained. And it may require a bit more patience. But it can be done. And you will do it.

CHAPTER SIXTEEN: Staying Safe: Crime, Cops, and Common Sense (It's Not *That* Dangerous)

Right, let's talk about safety. You're moving to a new country, a tiny island in the middle of the Mediterranean, and you're probably wondering if it's safe. Is Malta a haven for pickpockets? Are there gangs roaming the streets? Will you be kidnapped by pirates and held for ransom? Relax. The answer, in short, is that Malta is generally a very safe place. Violent crime is rare, and the biggest threat you're likely to face is sunburn or a *pastizz*-induced food coma.

But, like anywhere in the world, Malta is not crime-free. Petty theft, such as pickpocketing and bag snatching, can occur, especially in tourist areas and crowded places. There are also occasional reports of burglaries, car theft, and vandalism. And, like anywhere, there are areas that are considered less safe than others, especially at night. So, while Malta is generally safe, it's important to be aware of your surroundings, take sensible precautions, and use your common sense.

Think of Maltese safety as a sliding scale. At one end, you have the idyllic villages and rural areas, where the biggest danger is probably tripping over a sleeping cat. At the other end, you have Paceville, the nightlife district in St. Julian's, where the biggest dangers are drunken tourists, overpriced drinks, and the occasional bar fight. Most of Malta falls somewhere in the middle, with a level of safety that's comparable to most other European countries.

The Malta Police Force is responsible for maintaining law and order on the islands. They're generally visible and approachable, and they're usually happy to help if you have a problem. The police officers are mostly Maltese, but many of them speak English, especially in the tourist areas. You'll see them patrolling the streets, directing traffic, and responding to incidents. They're not always the most efficient or the most proactive police force, but they're generally reliable.

The emergency number in Malta is 112, the same as in the rest of Europe. You can call this number to contact the police, the ambulance service, or the fire department. The operators speak English, and they'll dispatch the appropriate service to your location. It's a good idea to save this number in your phone, just in case you need it. Hopefully, you won't, but it's always better to be prepared. Just dial the number and ask.

If you're the victim of a crime, you should report it to the police as soon as possible. You can do this by calling 112 or by visiting a police station. The police will take a statement from you and investigate the incident. It's important to provide as much detail as possible, including the time, location, and description of any suspects. The police might not always be able to recover your stolen property or catch the perpetrator, but it's important to report the crime nonetheless.

Petty theft is the most common type of crime in Malta, especially in tourist areas like Valletta, Sliema, and St. Julian's. Pickpockets and bag snatchers often target crowded places, such as buses, markets, and beaches. They're usually quick and skillful, and you might not even realize you've been robbed until it's too late. The best way to protect yourself is to be aware of your surroundings, keep your valuables close to you, and avoid carrying large amounts of cash.

Consider using a money belt or a cross-body bag that's difficult to snatch. Keep your phone and wallet in a secure pocket, and don't leave your belongings unattended, especially on the beach or in a crowded cafe. If you're traveling on a bus, keep your bag on your lap or between your feet, and be wary of anyone who seems to be getting too close to you. It's all about being vigilant and taking sensible precautions.

Burglaries can occur in Malta, although they're not as common as petty theft. Burglars often target empty houses or apartments, especially during the holiday season when people are away. The best way to protect your home is to make it look occupied, even when you're not there. Use timers to turn lights on and off, ask a neighbor to collect your mail, and don't post your travel plans on social media. And invest in locks.

It's also a good idea to install a burglar alarm and to secure all windows and doors. If you're renting an apartment, check with your landlord to see if there's an existing alarm system. If you're buying a property, consider investing in a good quality security system. It's an extra expense, but it can provide peace of mind and deter potential burglars. It might even reduce your home insurance premium, and will make you feel safer.

Car theft and vandalism are also a concern in Malta, although they're not as widespread as in some other European countries. Thieves often target cars parked in poorly lit areas or in isolated spots. The best way to protect your car is to park in a well-lit, secure area, and to avoid leaving valuables in plain sight. Consider installing a car alarm and a steering wheel lock, and always lock your car doors and windows, even when you're just popping into a shop.

If you're renting a car in Malta, make sure it's from a reputable company and that it has adequate insurance coverage. Check the car carefully for any existing damage before you drive away, and take photos if necessary. Report any damage to the rental company immediately, and keep a copy of the rental agreement and any other relevant documents. It's always better to be safe than sorry, especially when dealing with rental cars.

Paceville, the nightlife district in St. Julian's, is generally considered to be less safe than other parts of Malta, especially at night. There are numerous bars, clubs, and restaurants in the area, and it attracts a large number of tourists and young people. The combination of alcohol, crowds, and late-night revelry can sometimes lead to problems, such as fights, pickpocketing, and drug-related incidents. It is best avoided, at night particularly.

If you're going out in Paceville, it's important to be aware of your surroundings and to take precautions. Stick with your friends, don't accept drinks from strangers, and avoid walking alone in dark or isolated areas. If you feel uncomfortable or unsafe, leave the area and go somewhere else. There are plenty of other places to enjoy a night out in Malta without putting yourself at risk. The risks are not that high.

Drug use is illegal in Malta, and the police take a strict approach to drug-related offenses. Possession of even small amounts of drugs can lead to arrest and prosecution. The penalties for drug trafficking are severe, including long prison sentences. It's best to avoid any involvement with drugs while you're in Malta, and to be wary of anyone who offers you drugs or tries to involve you in drug-related activities. You do not want any trouble.

Prostitution is also illegal in Malta, although it does exist, particularly in certain areas of Paceville and Marsa. Soliciting or engaging in prostitution can lead to arrest and prosecution. It's best to avoid any involvement with prostitution while you're in Malta, and to be wary of anyone who approaches you in a suspicious manner. The police do conduct regular patrols in areas where prostitution is known to occur. You do not want that trouble either.

While Malta is generally a safe country, there are certain areas that are considered to be less safe than others, especially at night. These areas include parts of Marsa, Hamrun, and some of the inner harbor areas. These areas are not necessarily dangerous, but they tend to have higher rates of crime and social problems. It's best to avoid these areas at night, especially if you're alone, and to be extra cautious if you do need to go there.

One of the things that makes Malta generally safe is the strong sense of community. In the villages, especially, people know their neighbors, and they look out for each other. There's a sense of belonging and a shared responsibility for maintaining safety and security. This can be a great comfort for expats, especially those who are feeling vulnerable or isolated. It's a welcoming environment, and it's one of the things that makes Malta a special place to live.

The Maltese are generally quite law-abiding, and they have a strong respect for authority. This is partly due to the influence of the Catholic Church, which has traditionally played a significant role in Maltese society. It's also due to the small size of the country, where everyone knows everyone, and there's a strong sense of social control. This doesn't mean that crime doesn't occur, but it does mean that it's generally less tolerated than in some other countries.

One of the things that can surprise expats is the number of CCTV cameras in Malta. You'll see them everywhere, from the streets and shops to the buses and public buildings. The cameras are there to deter crime and to provide evidence in case of an incident. Some people find the presence of CCTV cameras reassuring, while others find it intrusive. It's a matter of personal preference, but it's a reality of life in Malta.

Another thing that can surprise expats is the number of fireworks displays in Malta. As mentioned earlier, the Maltese love fireworks, and they're used to celebrate all sorts of occasions, from village *festas* to weddings and football victories. The fireworks displays can be spectacular, but they can also be incredibly loud, and they can go on for hours. If you're sensitive to noise, you might want to check the local *festa* schedule and avoid those areas during the celebrations.

While Malta is generally a safe place, it's important to be aware of the potential risks and to take sensible precautions. Don't be complacent, and don't assume that because crime is rare, it won't happen to you. Use your common sense, be aware of your surroundings, and take steps to protect yourself and your belongings. It's all about being proactive and taking responsibility for your own safety. And you are responsible for your own safety.

If you're concerned about safety in Malta, you can check the latest crime statistics and travel advisories from your home country's government. These resources can provide up-to-date information on any specific risks or threats, and they can offer advice on how to stay safe. However, it's important to remember that these resources often focus on the negative aspects of a country, and they might not give a complete picture of the overall safety situation.

One of the best ways to stay safe in Malta is to connect with the local community and to get to know your neighbors. The Maltese are generally friendly and helpful, and they can be a valuable source of information and support. They can tell you about any local safety concerns, and they can offer advice on how to avoid problems. They can also keep an eye on your property when you're away, and they can be a first point of contact in case of an emergency.

Malta is generally a safe and welcoming country, and most expats have a positive experience living there. However, like anywhere in the world, crime can occur, and it's important to be aware of the potential risks and to take sensible precautions. By using your common sense, being vigilant, and connecting with the local community, you can minimize the risks and enjoy a safe and fulfilling life in Malta. Just don't wander around Paceville drunk at 3 am.

One specific thing that is worth being aware of is the risk of scams. Like many countries, Malta has its share of scams, and these are often aimed at tourists and expats. They may involve offers of goods or services, often at very low prices, which turn out to be fraudulent. Or they may involve requests for money for various reasons. The key thing is to be aware and not get drawn in.

If something sounds too good to be true, it probably is. So be careful. And do not give money to people you don't know, for any reason. It is very unlikely to be genuine. And do not give out personal information, such as bank details, to people who contact you unexpectedly. This is particularly important if you are contacted by phone or email. Be very careful, and check the details.

Another thing to be aware of is the risk of road accidents. As has been mentioned, Maltese driving can be a little, shall we say, erratic. So be careful on the roads, whether you are driving, cycling or walking. Always pay attention, and be aware of other road users. There are many accidents in Malta, and you do not want to be involved in one. So take care on the roads at all times.

Overall, however, Malta is a safe place. Crime rates are relatively low, and violent crime is rare. But it is always important to be aware, and to take precautions. And to use your common sense. If you do these things, you should have a safe and enjoyable time in Malta. And you should not have any problems. Just be sensible, and take the necessary precautions.

So don't worry too much about safety in Malta. It is probably safer than where you are coming from. But, as in any country, you should be aware of your surroundings. You should take precautions. And you should not take unnecessary risks. If you follow this advice, you will in all probability have a safe and enjoyable time during your Maltese adventure.

CHAPTER SEVENTEEN: Pets: Bringing Your Furry (or Scaly) Friend to Paradise

So, you're dreaming of Maltese sunsets, *pastizzi*-fueled adventures, and... your beloved pet frolicking on the beach beside you? Excellent! Malta can be a wonderful place for pets, with plenty of sunshine, outdoor space (depending on where you live), and a generally pet-friendly culture. However, bringing your furry, feathered, or scaled companion to a new country involves more than just booking an extra seat on the plane. Prepare for paperwork, regulations, and a few uniquely Maltese quirks.

Think of bringing your pet to Malta as a mini-version of your own relocation process. There are rules, regulations, forms to fill out, and potential headaches to navigate. But, unlike the visa process, this one comes with the added responsibility of ensuring your pet's well-being and safety throughout the journey. It's not just about ticking boxes; it's about making sure your best friend arrives in Malta happy, healthy, and ready to embrace the island life. So it's even more important.

First, the good news: Malta is part of the EU Pet Travel Scheme, which means that bringing pets from other EU countries is relatively straightforward. The basic requirements include a microchip, a valid rabies vaccination (administered *after* the microchip), and an EU Pet Passport. The Pet Passport is a standardized document that contains your pet's identification details, vaccination records, and other relevant information. It's issued by a veterinarian, and it's essential for traveling with your pet within the EU.

If you're coming from a non-EU country, the process is a bit more complicated, and the specific requirements vary depending on the country of origin. You'll likely need a health certificate issued by a veterinarian in your home country, confirming that your pet is free from infectious diseases and fit to travel. You might also need to provide proof of a rabies antibody titration test, which measures the level of rabies antibodies in your pet's blood. This test needs to be done a specific time after the rabies vaccination.

Regardless of where you're coming from, it's crucial to start the process well in advance of your move. Some of the requirements, such as the rabies antibody titration test, can take several weeks or even months to complete. You'll also need to factor in time for booking flights, arranging pet transport, and dealing with any unexpected delays. The sooner you start, the smoother the process will be, both for you and your pet. Plan the details in advance.

The Maltese authorities are quite strict about enforcing the pet import regulations, and they can refuse entry to animals that don't meet the requirements. This can be heartbreaking, and it can also be very expensive, as you'll be responsible for the cost of returning your pet to your home country or placing them in quarantine. So, double-check, triple-check, and quadruple-check that you have all the necessary documentation and that your pet meets all the requirements before you travel.

Once you've sorted out the paperwork, you'll need to decide how your pet will travel to Malta. The most common option is to fly, either in the cabin with you (if your pet is small enough) or as cargo. Some airlines allow small pets to travel in the cabin, provided they're in an approved carrier that fits under the seat in front of you. However, there are restrictions on the size and weight of the pet, and the number of pets allowed per flight is limited.

If your pet is too large to travel in the cabin, they'll need to travel as cargo. This means they'll be transported in a special, pressurized compartment in the hold of the aircraft. It's generally safe, but it can be stressful for pets, especially if they're not used to traveling. It's important to choose an airline with a good reputation for pet transport and to follow their guidelines carefully. You should also ensure that your pet is comfortable and well-prepared.

You can also use a pet transport company to handle the logistics of your pet's move. These companies specialize in transporting animals, and they can take care of everything from booking flights and arranging veterinary checks to providing crates and handling customs clearance. It's a more expensive option than doing it yourself, but it can be worth it if you're feeling overwhelmed by the process or if you have a pet with special needs.

Before your pet travels, you'll need to get them used to their carrier or crate. This is especially important if they're traveling as cargo, as they'll be spending several hours in the crate. Start by introducing the crate gradually, making it a positive and comfortable space for your pet. Put their favorite toys and blankets inside, and feed them meals in the crate. Gradually increase the amount of time they spend in the crate, and take them on short car journeys to get them used to the motion.

On the day of travel, make sure your pet has had a chance to exercise and relieve themselves before going to the airport. Avoid feeding them a large meal right before the flight, as this can cause stomach upset. Provide them with water, but don't overdo it, as they won't be able to relieve themselves during the flight. And, most importantly, try to stay calm and relaxed yourself, as your pet can sense your anxiety.

When you arrive in Malta, your pet will be checked by a veterinarian at the airport. They'll examine your pet's documents, check their microchip, and ensure that they're healthy and fit to enter the country. If everything is in order, your pet will be released to you, and you can finally start your Maltese adventure together. If there are any problems with the documentation or your pet's health, they might be quarantined or even refused entry.

Once your pet is settled in Malta, you'll need to register them with a local veterinarian. This is important for routine check-ups, vaccinations, and any emergency medical care your pet might need. There are numerous veterinarians in Malta, and many of them speak English. Ask for recommendations from other expats or check online reviews to find a vet that you feel comfortable with. It is important to have a professional to turn to.

You'll also need to familiarize yourself with the local regulations regarding pets. In Malta, dogs must be licensed and microchipped, and they must be kept on a leash in public areas, except in designated dog parks. There are also restrictions on certain breeds of dogs, and some breeds are banned altogether. It's important to check the latest regulations with your local council and to ensure that you're complying with all the rules.

Malta is generally a pet-friendly country, but there are some places where pets are not allowed, such as certain beaches, restaurants, and shops. Look for signs indicating whether pets are permitted, and respect the rules. If you're unsure, it's always best to ask. Most Maltese people are understanding, but it's important to be considerate of others and to avoid causing any inconvenience. And common sense should prevail.

One of the joys of having a pet in Malta is the opportunity to explore the island's outdoor spaces together. There are numerous parks, beaches, and hiking trails where you can take your dog for a walk or a run. Just be aware of the heat, especially during the summer months. Avoid walking your dog during the hottest part of the day, and make sure they have access to plenty of water. And, of course, clean up after your dog.

Malta also has a growing number of dog-friendly cafes and restaurants, where you can enjoy a meal or a drink with your furry friend by your side. These establishments often provide water bowls and even dog treats. It's a great way to socialize with other pet owners and to enjoy the Maltese lifestyle with your companion. Just make sure your dog is well-behaved and doesn't disturb other patrons.

If you're planning to rent a property in Malta, it's important to check whether pets are allowed. Some landlords are happy to accept pets, while others have strict no-pet policies. Be upfront about your pet when you're looking for a property, and make sure it's clearly stated in the rental agreement. You might need to pay an additional deposit to cover any potential damage caused by your pet.

If you're planning to travel within Malta or to other EU countries with your pet, you'll need to ensure that their vaccinations are up to date and that their Pet Passport is valid. It's always a good idea to check the specific requirements of the country you're visiting, as they can vary. And, of course, make sure your pet is comfortable and safe during the journey. You should plan ahead.

Bringing your pet to Malta can be a rewarding experience, but it requires careful planning and preparation. By following the regulations, taking care of your pet's needs, and being a responsible pet owner, you can ensure that your furry, feathered, or scaled friend enjoys a happy and healthy life in their new Maltese home. And you'll have a loyal companion to share your adventures with, from exploring ancient ruins to lounging on the beach.

One thing to be aware of is that stray animals, particularly cats, are common in Malta. Many of these animals are feral, meaning they're not socialized to humans, but some are abandoned pets. There are several animal welfare organizations in Malta that work to rescue, rehabilitate, and rehome stray animals. If you're considering getting a pet in Malta, consider adopting a rescue animal instead of buying from a breeder.

If you encounter a stray animal that appears to be injured or in distress, you can contact one of the animal welfare organizations for assistance. They can provide advice and, in some cases, rescue the animal and provide it with veterinary care. However, it's important to be cautious when approaching stray animals, as they might be frightened or aggressive. Don't put yourself at risk, and don't attempt to handle an animal unless you're confident that it's safe to do so.

Another thing to be aware of is that certain pests, such as fleas, ticks, and mosquitoes, are common in Malta, especially during the warmer months. These pests can transmit diseases to your pet, so it's important to take preventative measures. Talk to your veterinarian about the best flea and tick control products for your pet, and consider using a mosquito repellent if you're spending time outdoors in the evening.

Leishmaniasis is a serious disease that's transmitted by sandflies, which are common in Malta. The disease can affect dogs, cats, and humans, and it can be fatal if left untreated. There's no vaccine for leishmaniasis, but there are preventative measures you can take to protect your pet. These include using insect repellent, avoiding walking your dog at dawn and dusk when sandflies are most active, and keeping your pet indoors during the evening.

If you're concerned about leishmaniasis, talk to your veterinarian. They can advise you on the best preventative measures for your pet and monitor them for any signs of the disease. Early detection and treatment are crucial for managing leishmaniasis, so it's important to be vigilant and to seek veterinary care if you notice any unusual symptoms in your pet. It is important to be well informed on such matters.

Bringing your pet to Malta is a big decision, but it can be a wonderful experience for both you and your animal companion. With careful planning, preparation, and a bit of patience, you can navigate the regulations, ensure your pet's well-being, and enjoy a fulfilling life together in this beautiful Mediterranean island. Just remember to pack the sunscreen, the *pastizzi*, and, of course, the pet treats. You are bringing your family to Malta.

One final consideration that should be taken into account is the cost. Bringing a pet to Malta is not cheap. There are the costs of vaccinations, microchips, pet passports, and health certificates. There are the costs of flights and transport. And there may be quarantine costs, if there is an issue. So be prepared for these costs.

But it is worth it, to bring your pet with you to Malta. To have your furry friend with you is part of your new life. And they will help you to settle in. So take care of the details, be prepared for the process, and look forward to the time when you and your pet are settled in to your new Maltese life.

CHAPTER EIGHTEEN: Utilities: Power Cuts, Water Pressure, and the Joys of Island Living

Alright, let's talk about the less glamorous side of island life: utilities. You know, those essential services that you take for granted until they suddenly disappear, leaving you in the dark, sweating profusely, and wondering if you accidentally time-traveled back to the Stone Age. In Malta, utilities can be an adventure, a test of your patience, and a source of endless amusement (or frustration, depending on your perspective). It is not quite the Stone Age.

Think of Maltese utilities as a quirky old house. It has character, it has history, but it also has its share of creaky pipes, flickering lights, and mysterious noises. Sometimes everything works perfectly, and you enjoy a seamless flow of electricity, water, and internet. Other times, well, let's just say you might find yourself lighting candles, showering with a trickle of water, and cursing the day you decided to move to a rock in the Mediterranean.

Let's start with electricity. The electricity supply in Malta is generally reliable, but power cuts do happen. They're more common during the summer months, when the demand for air conditioning is at its peak, and they can also occur during storms or due to maintenance work. The power cuts are usually short, lasting from a few minutes to a few hours, but they can be disruptive, especially if you're working from home or relying on electrical appliances.

The electricity provider in Malta is Enemalta, a state-owned company that has a monopoly on the distribution of electricity. The voltage is 230V, and the frequency is 50Hz, the same as in most of Europe. The plugs and sockets are the three-pin type, the same as in the UK. If you're coming from a country with a different voltage or plug type, you'll need to use an adapter or a converter.

The cost of electricity in Malta can be quite high, especially during the summer months. This is due to the widespread use of air conditioning and the fact that Malta relies heavily on imported fossil fuels for electricity generation. There are different tariffs available, and the price per unit varies depending on your consumption and the time of day. It's a good idea to be mindful of your electricity usage and to take steps to conserve energy.

One way to reduce your electricity bill is to use energy-efficient appliances. Look for appliances with a high energy efficiency rating (A+++ is the best), and avoid leaving appliances on standby when you're not using them. You can also use energy-saving light bulbs, such as LEDs, which use significantly less electricity than traditional incandescent bulbs. And, of course, try to limit your use of air conditioning, especially during the hottest part of the day.

Another way to save on electricity is to take advantage of Malta's abundant sunshine. Consider installing solar panels on your roof, which can generate electricity and reduce your reliance on the grid. There are government incentives available for solar panel installations, and it can be a good long-term investment, especially if you own your property. It's also a more environmentally friendly option than relying solely on fossil fuels.

If you experience a power cut, the first thing to do is to check if it's a localized problem or a more widespread outage. Check if your neighbors have power, and look for any announcements from Enemalta on their website or social media. If it's a localized problem, check your circuit breaker to see if a fuse has blown. If it's a more widespread outage, there's not much you can do except wait for the power to be restored.

It's a good idea to have a backup plan for power cuts, especially if you rely on electricity for essential appliances, such as a refrigerator or a medical device. Consider investing in a uninterruptible power supply (UPS), which can provide temporary power to your devices during a power cut. You can also keep a supply of candles, flashlights, and batteries on hand, just in case. And, of course, make sure your phone is fully charged.

Now, let's move on to water. Water is a precious resource in Malta, as the island has limited natural freshwater sources. Most of the water supply comes from desalination plants, which convert seawater into potable water. The desalination process is energy-intensive, and it contributes to the relatively high cost of water in Malta. It's important to be mindful of your water usage and to avoid wasting water unnecessarily. But it is good water.

The water supply in Malta is generally safe to drink, but some people prefer to use bottled water or a water filter, especially in older buildings where the pipes might be corroded. The water pressure can vary, especially in older buildings and during peak hours. You might experience a weak shower or a slow-filling toilet, which can be frustrating. There's not much you can do about it, except to adapt to the Maltese way of life.

The water provider in Malta is the Water Services Corporation (WSC), another state-owned company. The water bills are usually issued every two months, and they're based on your consumption. There are different tariffs available, and the price per unit varies depending on your usage. It's a good idea to check your water meter regularly to monitor your consumption and to detect any leaks. A dripping tap can waste a surprising amount of water.

One way to conserve water is to take shorter showers and to avoid leaving the tap running while you're brushing your teeth or washing dishes. You can also install water-saving devices, such as low-flow showerheads and dual-flush toilets. If you have a garden, consider using a rainwater harvesting system to collect rainwater for watering your plants. It's a more sustainable option than using tap water, and it can help to reduce your water bill.

If you experience a water outage, the first thing to do is to check if it's a localized problem or a more widespread issue. Check if your neighbors have water, and look for any announcements from the WSC on their website or social media. If it's a localized problem, check your main water valve to see if it's been accidentally turned off. If it's a more widespread outage, there's not much you can do except wait for the water to be restored.

It's a good idea to keep a supply of bottled water on hand, just in case of a water outage. You can also fill up some containers with water before a scheduled outage, if you know about it in advance. And, of course, try to conserve water as much as possible, even when there's no outage. Every drop counts, especially on a small island with limited water resources. It is important to be sensible.

Now, let's talk about internet and telecommunications. Malta has a relatively well-developed telecommunications infrastructure, with several providers offering a range of services, including broadband internet, mobile phone services, and television packages. The internet speed and reliability can vary depending on your location and the provider you choose. Some areas have excellent fiber-optic connections, while others are still stuck with slower ADSL technology. There is a good choice.

The main telecommunications providers in Malta are GO, Melita, and Vodafone. They offer a range of packages, from basic internet-only plans to bundled packages that include television and mobile phone services. It's a good idea to compare the different providers and their offerings to find the best deal for your needs. Consider the speed, the data allowance, the contract length, and the customer service reputation of each provider.

The cost of internet and telecommunications in Malta is generally reasonable, compared to other European countries. However, it can vary depending on the package you choose and the provider you select. It's a good idea to shop around and to negotiate with the providers to get the best possible price. And don't be afraid to switch providers if you're not happy with the service you're receiving.

One thing to be aware of is that the internet speed advertised by the providers might not always be the actual speed you experience. This is due to various factors, such as the distance from your home to the nearest exchange, the quality of the wiring in your building, and the number of people using the internet at the same time. It's a good idea to test your internet speed regularly to see if you're getting what you're paying for.

If you're experiencing slow internet speeds or frequent disconnections, there are several things you can try. First, check your router and modem to make sure they're working properly. Restart them, and check all the cables to make sure they're securely connected. You can also try moving your router to a different location, as the signal strength can vary depending on the placement.

If the problem persists, contact your internet provider and report the issue. They might be able to troubleshoot the problem remotely or send a technician to your home to check the connection. It might take some time to resolve the issue, but be persistent and don't give up. A reliable internet connection is essential for modern life, especially if you're working from home or relying on online services.

Mobile phone coverage in Malta is generally good, with several providers offering 4G and 5G services. The main providers are GO, Melita, and Vodafone, the same as for internet and television. They offer a range of prepaid and postpaid plans, with different data allowances, call minutes, and text messages. It's a good idea to compare the different plans and choose one that suits your needs and budget.

If you're coming from another EU country, you can use your mobile phone in Malta without incurring roaming charges, thanks to the EU's "roam like at home" rules. This means you can use your data allowance, call minutes, and text messages as you would in your home country. However, there are some fair usage limits, so it's a good idea to check the terms and conditions of your mobile phone plan.

If you're coming from a non-EU country, you'll likely incur roaming charges if you use your mobile phone in Malta. The charges can be quite high, especially for data usage. It's a good idea to check with your mobile phone provider before you travel and to consider purchasing a local SIM card when you arrive in Malta. A local SIM card will give you a Maltese phone number and access to local rates, which are usually much cheaper than roaming charges.

Waste collection is another utility service that you'll need to deal with in Malta. The waste collection system is managed by the local councils, and the specific rules and schedules vary depending on your locality. Generally, waste is collected on specific days of the week, and you'll need to separate your waste into different bags or bins: organic waste, recyclable waste (paper, plastic, metal, glass), and general waste. And you should follow this system.

The organic waste is collected in white bags or bins, the recyclable waste is collected in green or grey bags or bins, and the general waste is collected in black bags or bins. The specific colors and types of bags or bins might vary depending on your locality, so it's important to check with your local council. You'll also need to find out the collection days for your area and to put your waste out on the correct day.

Recycling is encouraged in Malta, and there are penalties for not separating your waste correctly. It's important to familiarize yourself with the local recycling rules and to make an effort to recycle as much as possible. It's good for the environment, and it can also help to reduce the amount of waste that goes to landfill. There are also bring-in sites located throughout the islands, where you can dispose of larger items.

Dealing with utilities in Malta can be a bit of a learning curve, but it's all part of the adventure of living on a small island. Be prepared for the occasional power cut, the fluctuating water pressure, and the sometimes-slow internet speeds. But also appreciate the abundance of sunshine, the access to clean water, and the relatively well-developed telecommunications infrastructure. It's all about finding a balance and adapting to the Maltese way of life.

CHAPTER NINETEEN: Shopping: From Supermarkets to Souks (and Haggling Like a Pro)

Right, you've found a place to live, sorted out the utilities (mostly), and you're ready to stock your cupboards with something other than emergency *pastizzi*. It's time to tackle the Maltese shopping scene. Forget sterile hypermarkets and predictable chain stores; shopping in Malta is a sensory experience, a blend of modern convenience and traditional charm, with a dash of chaotic haggling thrown in for good measure. It is an experience.

Think of Maltese shopping as a treasure hunt. You might find exactly what you're looking for in a familiar supermarket, or you might stumble upon a hidden gem in a tiny village shop, a bustling market, or even a roadside stall. You'll encounter everything from designer boutiques and international brands to family-run businesses selling local crafts and produce. It's a diverse and often surprising landscape, and it's all part of the fun.

Let's start with the basics: supermarkets. Malta has a mix of local and international supermarket chains, offering a wide range of groceries, household goods, and other essentials. The main players are Lidl, Pavi, Pama, Scotts, and Wellbees, each with its own strengths and weaknesses. Lidl is generally the cheapest option, offering a range of discount products, but the selection can be limited. It is good for basics.

Pavi and Pama are larger supermarkets with a wider selection of goods, including imported items and specialty products. They're generally more expensive than Lidl, but they offer a more comprehensive shopping experience. Scotts and Wellbees are more upmarket supermarkets, offering a range of gourmet and organic products, as well as a more pleasant shopping environment. They're the most expensive option, but they're a good choice if you're looking for something special.

One thing you'll notice about Maltese supermarkets is that they're generally smaller than the hypermarkets you might be used to in other countries. This is due to the limited space on the island and the preference for smaller, more localized shops. The supermarkets can get crowded, especially on weekends and in the evenings, so be prepared for queues and a bit of a squeeze. It's all part of the Maltese shopping experience.

Another thing you'll notice is that the selection of products can vary significantly from what you're used to. Local produce, such as fruit, vegetables, bread, and cheese, is generally fresh and affordable. Imported goods, however, can be more expensive, and the availability can be inconsistent. You might find your favorite brand of cereal one week and then not see it again for months. It's a good idea to be flexible and to try local alternatives.

One of the perks of shopping in Malta is the abundance of fresh, local produce. The Maltese climate is ideal for growing a wide variety of fruits and vegetables, and you'll find them in abundance in supermarkets, markets, and roadside stalls. The produce is often seasonal, so you'll get the best flavors and the best prices when you buy what's in season. It's a great way to eat healthily and to support local farmers.

If you're looking for a more authentic shopping experience, head to one of Malta's many markets. The most famous is the Marsaxlokk fish market, held every Sunday in the picturesque fishing village of Marsaxlokk. It's a must-see for seafood lovers, with a wide variety of fresh fish and shellfish caught by local fishermen. It's a vibrant and colorful market, and it's a great place to experience the local culture.

The Valletta market, held daily in Merchant Street, is another popular market. It's a more general market, with vendors selling everything from fruits and vegetables to clothes, household goods, and souvenirs. It's a bustling and chaotic place, and it's a great place to practice your haggling skills. Just remember to be polite and respectful, and don't expect to get a huge discount. The Maltese are shrewd negotiators.

There are also numerous smaller markets held in towns and villages throughout Malta and Gozo. These markets often specialize in local crafts, produce, and antiques. They're a great place to find unique gifts and souvenirs, and to support local artisans and producers. Check the local listings to find out when and where the markets are held in your area. It is a great way to support local people.

If you're looking for clothes, shoes, and accessories, Malta offers a mix of international brands and local boutiques. Sliema and Valletta are the main shopping destinations, with a range of department stores, high-street chains, and designer boutiques. You'll find familiar brands like Zara, Mango, and Marks & Spencer, as well as a number of Italian and other European brands. The prices are generally in line with European averages.

There are also several shopping malls in Malta, such as The Point in Sliema, Bay Street in St. Julian's, and the Embassy Shopping Complex in Valletta. These malls offer a more modern shopping experience, with a mix of international and local brands, as well as restaurants, cafes, and cinemas. They're a good option if you're looking for a one-stop shopping destination, or if you want to escape the heat and humidity of the streets.

If you're looking for something a bit different, explore the smaller boutiques and independent shops in Valletta, Sliema, and other towns. You'll find unique clothing, jewelry, accessories, and homewares, often made by local designers and artisans. These shops are a great place to find one-of-a-kind items and to support the local creative community. They can be more expensive than the chain stores, but the quality is often higher.

One thing to be aware of is that the sizing of clothes and shoes can vary significantly in Malta. It's always a good idea to try things on before you buy them, especially if you're not familiar with the brand. The shop assistants are generally helpful and happy to assist you with finding the right size. Don't be afraid to ask for help, even if your Maltese is limited. You will find all sizes here.

If you're looking for souvenirs or gifts, Malta offers a wide range of options. Traditional Maltese crafts include lace, filigree jewelry, pottery, and blown glass. You'll find these items in souvenir shops, markets, and craft villages, such as the Ta' Qali Crafts Village near Mdina. It's a great place to find unique and authentic gifts, and to support local artisans. And it is a great place to spend time.

Another popular souvenir is Maltese food and drink. Local specialties include *pastizzi, ftira, ħobż biż-żejt*, honey, olive oil, wine, and liqueurs. You'll find these items in supermarkets, specialty food shops, and markets. They're a great way to take a taste of Malta home with you, and they make thoughtful gifts for friends and family. Just be aware of any restrictions on bringing food items into your home country.

Haggling is a common practice in Malta, especially in markets and small shops. It's considered perfectly acceptable to try to negotiate a lower price, and it's often expected. However, it's important to be polite and respectful, and to avoid being too aggressive. Start by offering a lower price than you're willing to pay, and be prepared to meet the seller somewhere in the middle. It's all part of the game.

The Maltese are generally shrewd negotiators, and they won't be easily fooled. Don't expect to get a huge discount, especially on items that are already reasonably priced. The goal is to reach a price that's fair to both you and the seller. It's a social interaction, and it's a way to build rapport with the locals. Just remember to smile, be friendly, and don't take it too seriously.

One thing to be aware of is that the opening hours of shops in Malta can be a bit unpredictable. Many shops close for a siesta in the afternoon, typically between 1 pm and 4 pm. They also tend to have shorter opening hours on Sundays and public holidays. It's a good idea to check the opening hours before you go, especially if you're traveling a long distance. It can be frustrating to arrive at a shop and find it closed.

If you're looking for a specific item and you can't find it in Malta, you can always try ordering it online. Many international retailers ship to Malta, although the shipping costs can be quite high. There are also a number of local online shops, offering a range of products, from groceries and household goods to clothes and electronics. It's a convenient option if you can't find what you're looking for in the physical shops.

One thing to be aware of is that consumer protection laws in Malta might be different from what you're used to in your home country. It's important to read the terms and conditions carefully before making a purchase, especially if you're buying something expensive or online. If you have a problem with a product or a service, you can contact the Malta Competition and Consumer Affairs Authority (MCCAA) for advice and assistance.

Shopping in Malta is an experience, a mix of modern convenience and traditional charm. It's a chance to explore the local culture, to interact with the Maltese people, and to discover unique and interesting products. It's not always the most efficient or the most predictable shopping experience, but it's always an adventure. So, embrace the chaos, practice your haggling skills, and enjoy the treasure hunt.

One of the things that often surprises expats is the prevalence of small, family-run shops in Malta. These shops often specialize in a particular type of product, such as hardware, stationery, or fabrics. They're a great place to find unique items and to get personalized service. The shopkeepers are usually knowledgeable about their products, and they're often happy to chat and offer advice. It is a more personalized experience.

These small shops are an important part of the Maltese economy and the local community. They're often passed down from generation to generation, and they represent a traditional way of life that's slowly disappearing in many other parts of the world. Supporting these small businesses is a way to contribute to the local economy and to preserve a unique aspect of Maltese culture. It is a more sustainable way to shop.

Another thing that often surprises expats is the lack of large department stores in Malta. While there are a few department stores in Sliema and Valletta, they're generally smaller and less comprehensive than the department stores you might be used to in other countries. This is due to the limited space on the island and the preference for smaller, more specialized shops. It's a different shopping experience, but it's one you'll quickly get used to.

If you're looking for a specific brand or a particular item, you might not always be able to find it in Malta. This is especially true for niche products or specialized equipment. You might need to order it online from another country, or you might need to find a local alternative. It's a good idea to be flexible and to be prepared to adapt to the local market. It is all part of living on a small island.

One of the advantages of shopping in Malta is that you'll often find unique and interesting products that you wouldn't find anywhere else. This is especially true for local crafts, food products, and souvenirs. You'll discover new flavors, new designs, and new ways of doing things. It's a chance to broaden your horizons and to experience something different. It is a more enriching experience.

Shopping in Malta is not just about buying things; it's about interacting with the local community and experiencing the Maltese way of life. It's about chatting with the shopkeepers, haggling with the market vendors, and discovering hidden gems in unexpected places. It's about slowing down, taking your time, and enjoying the process. It's a different way of shopping, and it's one that you might just grow to love.

One final consideration that is important is convenience. The Maltese often shop daily, buying fresh bread, and produce on a regular basis. This is often because their houses and apartments have limited storage, and smaller fridges. So, it is part of the Maltese way of life. And it is something you will need to adapt to.

It is also because the shops, markets, and other places to buy food are often located within walking distance. Or a short drive away.

So it is easy to shop in this way. And it can be a very enjoyable part of the day. It can also be a very sociable activity. So do not be afraid to change your ways.

Shopping in Malta can be different. But it can be an enjoyable experience. So do not try to expect it to be like shopping in your own country. Be prepared for it to be different. Embrace the difference. And enjoy it. It is all part of adjusting to your new life.

And you may well make new friends, and discover new things. You may well discover shops and stalls selling things that you did not expect. And you may well become a regular, and be welcomed. All this is possible. So get out there and start shopping. You will soon get used to the Maltese way.

CHAPTER TWENTY: Communications: Staying Connected (Without Breaking the Bank on Roaming Charges)

Right, you've made it to Malta. You're basking in the sunshine, stuffing your face with *pastizzi*, and maybe even mastering a few Maltese phrases. But there's one crucial element missing: staying connected. We're not talking about some spiritual awakening (though that might happen too); we're talking about phones, internet, and the ability to share your envy-inducing photos with the folks back home. Without ending up with a phone bill the size of a small island nation's GDP.

Think of Maltese communications as a three-layered cake. The bottom layer is mobile phones: essential for everyday life, navigating the island, and avoiding those dreaded roaming charges. The middle layer is internet: crucial for work, entertainment, and staying in touch with the outside world. And the top layer, the icing on the cake, is the postal service: surprisingly important for official documents, packages, and the occasional postcard to Aunt Mildred. It's a mix of modern technology, somewhat modern infrastructure, and a dash of "it's Malta, things work differently here."

Let's start with mobile phones. Your first instinct might be to simply use your existing phone and plan from your home country. *Mela*, hold your horses. Unless you're made of money, or you enjoy the thrill of financial ruin, roaming charges are your enemy. They're like tiny, invisible vampires, sucking the life out of your bank account with every call, text, and megabyte of data. The solution? Get a local SIM card. You don't want to be paying to call abroad.

Malta has three main mobile providers: GO, Melita, and Vodafone. They all offer a range of prepaid and postpaid plans, with varying amounts of data, call minutes, and text messages. The coverage is generally good across the islands, although there might be some black spots in rural areas or inside those thick-walled ancient buildings. The best provider for you will depend on your needs and usage patterns, so it's worth comparing their offerings.

Prepaid plans are a popular option for expats, as they offer flexibility and control over your spending. You simply buy a SIM card, top it up with credit, and use it until the credit runs out. You can top up online, at kiosks, or in shops throughout Malta. It's a straightforward system, and it avoids the risk of unexpected bills. However, the per-minute and per-megabyte rates might be higher than on postpaid plans. It's the more flexible option.

Postpaid plans, on the other hand, offer a fixed monthly fee and a set allowance of data, calls, and texts. They often come with additional benefits, such as discounted international calls or access to Wi-Fi hotspots. They're a good option if you're a heavy user or if you prefer the predictability of a fixed monthly bill. However, you'll need to sign a contract, and you might be subject to early termination fees if you decide to switch providers.

Getting a local SIM card is relatively easy. You can buy one at the airport upon arrival, or at any of the mobile providers' shops throughout Malta. You'll need to provide your passport or ID card for registration, and you might need to provide a local address. The SIM card will come with a Maltese phone number, which you'll need to give out to your contacts. You can then start using your phone as you normally would.

One thing to be aware of is that the cost of mobile data in Malta can be quite high, especially if you're using a prepaid plan and you're not careful. It's easy to burn through your data allowance quickly, especially if you're streaming videos, using social media, or making video calls. It's a good idea to monitor your data usage and to connect to Wi-Fi whenever possible to avoid unexpected charges.

Another thing to be aware of is that international calls from Malta can be expensive, especially if you're calling countries outside the EU. The mobile providers offer various international call packages, which can significantly reduce the cost. It's worth checking these out if you make frequent international calls. Alternatively, you can use internet-based calling services, such as Skype, WhatsApp, or Viber, which are generally much cheaper.

Now, let's move on to the internet. Having a reliable internet connection is essential for most expats, whether you're working remotely, studying online, or simply staying in touch with family and friends. Malta offers a range of internet options, from basic ADSL connections to high-speed fiber-optic broadband. The availability and speed of the internet can vary depending on your location, so it's important to check what's available in your area.

The main internet providers in Malta are GO, Melita, and Vodafone, the same as for mobile phones. They offer a range of packages, with varying speeds, data allowances, and contract lengths. It's a good idea to compare the different providers and their offerings to find the best deal for your needs. Consider the speed, the data allowance, the contract length, and the customer service reputation of each provider.

ADSL is the most basic type of internet connection, and it's generally the cheapest option. However, the speeds can be quite slow, especially in areas that are far from the telephone exchange. It's suitable for basic internet browsing and email, but it might not be sufficient for streaming videos or online gaming. If you're a heavy internet user, you'll probably want a faster connection. ADSL is still common.

Fiber-optic broadband is the fastest and most reliable type of internet connection available in Malta. It uses fiber-optic cables to transmit data, which allows for much higher speeds than ADSL. Fiber-optic broadband is ideal for streaming videos, online gaming, video conferencing, and other data-intensive activities. However, it's not available in all areas, and it's generally more expensive than ADSL. Check whether it is available in your area.

Another option is to use a mobile broadband connection. This involves using a mobile data SIM card in a portable router or a dongle, which creates a Wi-Fi hotspot that you can connect your devices to. It's a flexible option, as you can use it anywhere there's mobile coverage, but the speeds and data allowances can be limited. It's a good option if you're traveling frequently or if you don't have a fixed address.

The installation process for internet services can vary depending on the provider and the type of connection. For ADSL and fiber-optic connections, a technician will usually need to visit your home to install the necessary equipment and connect you to the network. This can take a few days or even a few weeks, depending on the provider's workload and the availability of technicians. It's a good idea to arrange the installation as soon as possible after you move in.

For mobile broadband connections, the setup is usually much simpler. You simply insert the SIM card into the router or dongle, and you're ready to go. However, you might need to configure the settings on your devices to connect to the Wi-Fi hotspot. The provider will usually provide instructions on how to do this, but it can be a bit tricky if you're not tech-savvy.

Once you're connected to the internet, it's important to take steps to protect your privacy and security. Use a strong password for your Wi-Fi network, and avoid using public Wi-Fi hotspots for sensitive activities, such as online banking or shopping. Install antivirus software on your devices, and be careful about clicking on links or downloading attachments from unknown sources. Cybercrime is a global problem, and Malta is no exception.

Now, let's talk about the postal service. In this digital age, you might think that the postal service is obsolete. But in Malta, it's still surprisingly important. You'll likely receive official documents, bills, and even the occasional package through the mail. And if you're sending anything internationally, you'll need to use the postal service or a courier company. The postal service is important to know about.

The postal service in Malta is operated by MaltaPost, a public company that provides a range of postal and courier services. The service is generally reliable, but it can be slow, especially for international mail. Letters and packages can take several days or even weeks to arrive, depending on the destination. If you're sending something urgent, it's best to use a courier service, such as DHL, FedEx, or UPS.

The post offices in Malta are generally open from Monday to Saturday, with shorter hours on Saturdays. You can buy stamps, send letters and packages, and collect registered mail at the post office. The staff usually speak English, and they're generally helpful. However, the post offices can get crowded, especially during peak hours, so be prepared for a bit of a wait. There may be queues involved.

If you're expecting a package, you'll usually receive a notification slip in your mailbox, informing you that the package is waiting for you at the post office. You'll need to bring the notification slip and your ID card to collect the package. If you're not home when the delivery is attempted, the postman might leave the package with a neighbor or try to deliver it again later.

One thing to be aware of is that the addressing system in Malta can be a bit confusing. Street names are often long and complicated, and house numbers are not always sequential. It's important to provide the full and correct address when sending or receiving mail, including the postcode. If you're unsure about the address, ask a local for help. They're usually happy to assist.

The cost of postal services in Malta is generally reasonable, compared to other European countries. The price depends on the weight and size of the item, and the destination. You can find the latest tariffs on the MaltaPost website. If you're sending something valuable or important, it's a good idea to use registered mail, which provides tracking and insurance.

Another thing to be aware of is that customs duties and taxes might apply to packages sent from outside the EU. The amount of duty and tax depends on the value and type of goods, and the country of origin. If you're receiving a package from outside the EU, you might need to pay these charges before the package is released to you. It's a good idea to check the customs regulations before ordering anything from outside the EU.

Staying connected in Malta is essential for both practical and social reasons. Whether you're making phone calls, browsing the internet, or sending a postcard to your loved ones, you'll need to navigate the Maltese communications landscape. It's a mix of modern technology and traditional methods, with its own set of quirks and challenges. But with a bit of planning and preparation, you can stay connected without breaking the bank.

One of the things that often surprises expats is the prevalence of landline phones in Malta. While mobile phones are ubiquitous, many Maltese households still have landline phones. This is partly due to tradition, and partly due to the fact that landline calls are often cheaper than mobile calls, especially for local calls. If you're making frequent calls within Malta, it might be worth considering getting a landline phone.

Another thing that often surprises expats is the popularity of television in Malta. While streaming services are gaining ground, traditional television is still a major form of entertainment. There are several local television channels, offering a mix of news, entertainment, and sports programming. Many Maltese households also have satellite or cable television, providing access to a wider range of international channels.

If you're a fan of television, you can subscribe to a television package from one of the main providers, such as GO, Melita, or Vodafone. The packages usually include a range of local and international channels, and you can often add on premium channels, such as sports or movie channels. The cost of television packages varies depending on the provider and the channels included.

Staying connected in Malta is not just about having access to phones, internet, and television. It's also about staying informed about what's happening in Malta and in the world. There are several English-language newspapers in Malta, such as the Times of Malta, The Malta Independent, and MaltaToday. These newspapers provide coverage of local and international news, as well as opinion pieces, sports, and entertainment.

You can also access news and information online, through the websites of the local newspapers and other news organizations. There are also several English-language news websites and blogs that focus specifically on Malta. These resources can be a valuable source of information for expats, providing insights into Maltese culture, politics, and society. And there are numerous ways to find them.

Social media is another important way to stay connected in Malta. Facebook, Instagram, and Twitter are widely used, and they're a great way to connect with other expats, to find out about local events and activities, and to stay informed about what's happening in Malta. There are numerous Facebook groups dedicated to expats in Malta, and these can be a valuable source of information, support, and social connections.

Staying connected in Malta is about more than just technology; it's about building relationships, engaging with the local community, and staying informed about the world around you. It's about finding a balance between staying connected to your home country and embracing your new life in Malta. It's about finding the right mix of communication tools and strategies that work for you.

One specific thing to consider is having a VPN. A virtual private network (VPN) can be useful in Malta for several reasons. It can enhance your online privacy and security, especially when using public Wi-Fi networks. It can also allow you to access geo-restricted content, such as streaming services or websites that are only available in certain countries. And it helps to avoid any censorship.

A VPN works by encrypting your internet traffic and routing it through a server in a different location. This makes it more difficult for third parties to track your online activity or to intercept your data. It also masks your IP address, which can help to protect your privacy. There are many VPN providers available, and it's important to choose a reputable one that offers good speeds and security features.

So staying connected in Malta is a multifaceted endeavor, involving technology, communication skills, and a willingness to adapt to the local way of doing things. It's about finding the right balance between staying in touch with your home country and embracing your new life in Malta. It's about using the available tools and resources to stay informed, entertained, and connected to the people and things that matter to you.

CHAPTER TWENTY-ONE: Driving in Malta: A Survival Guide (May Require a Therapist Afterwards)

Right, buckle up, buttercup. We're about to tackle the single most terrifying, exhilarating, and utterly baffling aspect of Maltese life: driving. Forget the history, the culture, the *pastizzi*; driving in Malta is a cultural experience unlike any other. It's a blend of Formula One racing, bumper cars, and a healthy dose of "hope for the best." It's not for the faint of heart, but with a bit of knowledge, a lot of patience, and a *very* good sense of humor, you might just survive.

Think of Maltese roads as a living organism. They're constantly changing, evolving, and throwing unexpected obstacles your way. One-way streets appear out of nowhere, road signs are more like suggestions, and roundabouts... well, we'll get to roundabouts. It's a chaotic, unpredictable system, and it requires a unique set of skills to navigate. You'll need the reflexes of a cat, the patience of a saint, and the audacity of a seasoned taxi driver.

First, the basics. As mentioned before, Malta drives on the left, like the UK, Australia, and a handful of other former British colonies. If you're coming from a country that drives on the right, this will take some getting used to. Your brain will scream at you to swerve into the wrong lane, your instincts will betray you, and you'll probably spend the first few weeks muttering "keep left, keep left" like a mantra.

The good news is that the human brain is remarkably adaptable. After a few days, or maybe a few weeks, driving on the left will start to feel normal. You'll stop having near-death experiences every time you approach a roundabout, and you'll even start to enjoy the challenge. Just remember to take it slow at first, practice in quiet areas, and don't be afraid to ask for help if you're feeling overwhelmed.

Now, about those roundabouts. Maltese roundabouts are legendary. They're not just traffic circles; they're swirling vortexes of chaos, where the rules of the road are more like guidelines, and the only certainty is that someone will cut you off. Think of them as a real-life game of chicken, where the winner is the driver who's most willing to risk life, limb, and their car's paint job. The faint-hearted need not apply.

The official rules of Maltese roundabouts are the same as in most other countries: give way to traffic already on the roundabout, and signal your exit. In practice, however, Maltese drivers have their own interpretation of these rules. They might enter the roundabout without yielding, exit from the wrong lane, or simply ignore all the rules altogether. It's a free-for-all, and you need to be prepared for anything. Best to be ready.

The key to surviving Maltese roundabouts is to be assertive, but not aggressive. You need to be confident enough to enter the roundabout when there's a gap, but you also need to be prepared to brake or swerve to avoid a collision. It's a delicate balance, and it takes practice to master. Don't be afraid to go around the roundabout a few times until you feel comfortable exiting. It's better to be safe than sorry.

Another challenge of driving in Malta is the narrow, winding streets, especially in the older towns and villages. You'll encounter roads that are barely wide enough for two cars to pass, let alone park. You'll need to be skilled at maneuvering in tight spaces, and you'll need to be patient, as you'll often encounter traffic jams and delays. It's a test of your driving skills and your ability to remain calm under pressure.

Parking in Malta is another adventure. Finding a parking space can feel like winning the lottery, especially in the central areas and during peak hours. You'll encounter cars parked in the most improbable places, double-parked, triple-parked, and even parked on the sidewalk. It's a chaotic free-for-all, and you need to be creative and resourceful to find a spot. Just be careful not to block traffic or obstruct pedestrian access.

There are designated parking areas in some towns and villages, but they're often full. You might need to circle around for a while until a space becomes available, or you might need to park further away and walk. It's a good idea to factor in extra time for parking, especially if you're going to a popular destination or an event. And be prepared to pay for parking in some areas. Be prepared to walk.

The Maltese driving style is, shall we say, *unique*. It's a blend of assertiveness, impatience, and a healthy disregard for the rules of the road. Maltese drivers are not afraid to honk their horns, tailgate, and overtake in questionable situations. They seem to have a sixth sense for anticipating traffic flow, and they're masters of squeezing through impossibly tight gaps. It's a style that can be intimidating for newcomers.

If you're used to a more cautious and rule-abiding driving style, you'll need to adjust your expectations in Malta. Don't be surprised if a driver cuts you off, pulls out in front of you without signaling, or ignores a stop sign. It's not necessarily personal; it's just the way they drive. Try to stay calm, don't take it personally, and focus on your own driving. It's all part of the experience.

One thing you'll notice is that the Maltese use their horns a lot. They use it to greet friends, to express frustration, to warn other drivers, and sometimes, it seems, just for the sheer joy of making noise. It's a constant soundtrack to the Maltese driving experience, and it can be a bit overwhelming at first. But you'll get used to it, and you might even find yourself using your horn more often than you used to.

Another thing you'll notice is that the Maltese are not big on indicating. They might signal their intentions at the last minute, or they might not signal at all. It's important to be aware of this and to anticipate their moves. Don't assume that a driver will turn just because they've indicated, and don't assume that they won't turn just because they haven't. It's all about being vigilant and prepared for anything.

Despite the challenges, driving in Malta can be a rewarding experience. It gives you the freedom to explore the island at your own pace, and it allows you to access areas that are difficult to reach by public transport. You'll discover hidden beaches, charming villages, and stunning viewpoints that you would otherwise miss. Just be prepared for the chaos, the narrow streets, and the, um, *creative* driving style of the Maltese.

If you're planning to drive in Malta, you'll need a valid driving license. If you have an EU/EEA license, you can use it in Malta without any restrictions. If you have a license from a non-EU/EEA country, you can use it for up to 12 months, after which you'll need to exchange it for a Maltese license. The process of exchanging your license involves filling out a form, providing some documents, and passing a practical driving test.

The Maltese driving test is notoriously difficult, and many expats fail it on their first attempt. It's not just about your driving skills; it's also about your knowledge of the Maltese Highway Code and your ability to navigate the unique challenges of Maltese roads. You'll be tested on your ability to handle roundabouts, your observation skills, and your overall awareness of other road users. It's a stressful experience.

If you're planning to buy a car in Malta, you'll need to register it with Transport Malta, the government agency responsible for road transport. You'll need to provide proof of ownership, your ID card, and a valid insurance certificate. You'll also need to pay the annual circulation tax, which is based on the age and emissions of your car. The process can be a bit bureaucratic, but it's generally straightforward.

Car insurance is mandatory in Malta, and there are several insurance providers offering a range of policies. It's important to compare the different policies and choose one that meets your needs and budget. Consider the level of coverage, the excess, and any additional benefits, such as roadside assistance. It's also a good idea to check the insurer's reputation for customer service and claims handling.

One thing to be aware of is that car theft and vandalism are not uncommon in Malta, especially in the more touristy areas. It's important to take precautions, such as parking in well-lit areas, not leaving valuables in your car, and considering installing an alarm system. It's also a good idea to have comprehensive car insurance that covers theft and vandalism. Prevention is better than cure, as they say.

Another thing to be aware of is that the roads in Malta can be quite rough, especially in the rural areas. You'll encounter potholes, uneven surfaces, and poorly maintained roads. It's important to drive carefully and to be aware of the road conditions. Avoid driving too fast, especially on unfamiliar roads, and be prepared to slow down or stop for obstacles. It's also a good idea to check your tires regularly.

Driving in Malta is an adventure, a challenge, and a cultural experience all rolled into one. It's not for the faint of heart, but it's also not as terrifying as some people make it out to be. With a bit of practice, a lot of patience, and a healthy dose of humor, you'll learn to navigate the Maltese roads and even enjoy the experience. Just remember to keep left, embrace the chaos, and don't be afraid to use your horn.

One of the best ways to improve your driving skills in Malta is to take a defensive driving course. Several driving schools offer these courses, which teach you how to anticipate hazards, avoid accidents, and handle challenging driving situations. It's a good investment, especially if you're new to driving on the left or if you're feeling nervous about driving in Malta. It can boost your confidence and make you a safer driver.

Another helpful tip is to use a GPS navigation system or a smartphone app to help you navigate. The roads in Malta can be confusing, especially in the older towns and villages, and it's easy to get lost. A GPS system can provide turn-by-turn directions, help you avoid traffic jams, and find parking spaces. It's a valuable tool, especially when you're exploring unfamiliar areas. It can be essential.

If you're not comfortable driving in Malta, or if you don't need a car for your daily commute, you can rely on public transport, taxis, or ride-hailing services. The bus system is extensive and affordable, although it can be unreliable. Taxis are readily available, but they're more expensive. Ride-hailing services, such as Bolt and eCabs, offer a convenient and often cheaper alternative to traditional taxis. It all depends on your needs.

One of the things that often surprises expats is the number of scooters and motorcycles on Maltese roads. They're a popular mode of transport, especially among young people, as they're relatively inexpensive, easy to park, and can weave through traffic. However, they can also be dangerous, especially in the hands of inexperienced riders. If you're driving a car, be extra cautious around scooters and motorcycles.

Another thing that often surprises expats is the number of old, classic cars on Maltese roads. Malta has a thriving classic car scene, and you'll often see vintage cars from the 1950s, 1960s, and 1970s being driven around. These cars are often lovingly restored and maintained by their owners, and they're a testament to the Maltese passion for automobiles. It's a unique aspect of Maltese culture.

Driving in Malta is a microcosm of Maltese life: chaotic, colorful, and full of surprises. It's a challenge, but it's also an opportunity to learn new skills, to adapt to a new environment, and to experience a different way of life. It's a journey that will test your patience, your nerves, and your sense of humor. But it's also a journey that will reward you with unforgettable experiences and a deeper appreciation for this quirky little island.

One final consideration that should be taken into account is the environment. Driving in Malta, particularly in older cars, contributes to air pollution. And the narrow roads and heavy traffic increase this. So you may want to consider alternative forms of transport for this reason. It is something to consider. And it is something you may want to think about, before committing to driving in Malta.

But overall, driving in Malta is an experience. And it is an experience that is worth having. And it may be a necessity, depending on where you live, and what you do. So be prepared for it. Be aware of the potential challenges. And most of all, be careful. The roads can be dangerous. But if you take care, you will be fine.

And before long, you may well find yourself driving like a local. Honking your horn, navigating the roundabouts, and squeezing through narrow gaps. And you may well find yourself enjoying it. It is all part of the Maltese experience. So embrace it. And be safe. And do not be surprised if you need to see a therapist afterwards.

CHAPTER TWENTY-TWO: Climate: Sun, Sun, and More Sun (and the Occasional Biblical Downpour)

Right, let's talk about the weather. You're moving to a Mediterranean island, so you're probably picturing endless sunshine, balmy breezes, and temperatures that rarely dip below "perfectly pleasant." And, for the most part, you'd be right. Malta boasts a climate that's the envy of most of Europe, with over 300 days of sunshine per year and mild winters. But, like everything in Malta, there's more to the story than meets the eye.

Think of the Maltese climate as a four-act play. Act One is Spring (March to May): a glorious period of warm sunshine, blooming flowers, and gentle breezes. It's arguably the best time to visit Malta, as the temperatures are comfortable, the crowds are smaller, and the landscape is at its most vibrant. You'll be able to enjoy outdoor activities without melting into a puddle of sweat, and you'll be able to sleep without the constant hum of the air conditioner.

Act Two is Summer (June to August): the main event, the headliner, the reason why most people flock to Malta. It's hot, it's dry, and it's sunny, with temperatures often soaring above 30°C (86°F) and sometimes even reaching 40°C (104°F). The sea is warm and inviting, the beaches are packed, and the air conditioning units are working overtime. It's a time for swimming, sunbathing, and embracing the siesta with a passion usually reserved for *pastizzi*.

Act Three is Autumn (September to November): a shoulder season that offers a welcome respite from the summer heat. The temperatures are still warm, but more manageable, and the sea remains swimmable well into October. The crowds have thinned out, and the prices have dropped, making it a great time to visit if you're looking for a more relaxed and affordable experience.

You'll still get plenty of sunshine, but you won't need to carry a portable fan everywhere you go.

Act Four is Winter (December to February): the quietest and mildest season, with temperatures averaging around 15°C (59°F). It's not exactly beach weather, but it's still pleasant enough for outdoor activities, especially on sunny days. You'll encounter some rain, and the occasional storm, but the winters are generally short and mild compared to most of Europe. It's a time for exploring historical sites, enjoying cozy cafes, and appreciating the tranquility of the off-season.

The star of the show, of course, is the sun. The Maltese sun is strong, intense, and ever-present. It's the reason why the island is bathed in a golden light, why the sea sparkles so invitingly, and why sunscreen is your best friend. You'll need to protect yourself from the sun's rays year-round, even on cloudy days. Wear sunscreen, a hat, and sunglasses, and avoid spending too much time in direct sunlight during the hottest part of the day.

The sun's intensity can be deceptive, especially if you're coming from a cooler climate. You might not feel the heat as much as you expect, due to the sea breeze and the relatively low humidity. But the UV index can be very high, and you can easily get sunburned without realizing it. So, be cautious, be prepared, and don't underestimate the power of the Maltese sun. It's a force to be reckoned with.

The humidity in Malta can vary depending on the season and the wind direction. During the summer months, the humidity is generally low, which makes the heat more bearable. However, when the wind blows from the south, bringing air from North Africa, the humidity can increase significantly, making it feel much hotter than the actual temperature. This is known as the *Xlokk* (Sirocco) wind, and it can be quite uncomfortable.

The *Xlokk* wind can also bring with it fine sand and dust from the Sahara Desert, creating a hazy atmosphere and coating everything in a thin layer of red dust. It's not the most pleasant experience, but it's a reminder of Malta's proximity to Africa and the influence of the desert climate. If you suffer from respiratory problems, it's a good idea to stay indoors during a *Xlokk* wind.

The sea plays a crucial role in regulating the Maltese climate. The Mediterranean Sea acts as a giant heat sink, absorbing heat during the summer and releasing it slowly during the winter. This moderates the temperatures, preventing them from becoming too extreme. The sea also provides a refreshing breeze, especially during the summer months, which helps to make the heat more bearable. It's one of the reasons why Malta is such a popular destination.

Rainfall in Malta is concentrated in the winter months, from October to March. The average annual rainfall is around 600mm (24 inches), which is significantly less than in many other European countries. However, the rain can be quite heavy when it does fall, and it can lead to localized flooding, especially in low-lying areas. The Maltese are used to these downpours, and they often joke about the "biblical" nature of the rain.

The storms in Malta can be quite dramatic, with strong winds, thunder, and lightning. They usually pass quickly, leaving behind clear skies and fresh air. But they can also cause disruptions to transport, power outages, and even damage to buildings. It's important to be aware of the weather forecast and to take precautions during storms. Stay indoors, avoid driving, and secure any loose objects that could be blown away.

One of the things that often surprises visitors is how quickly the weather can change in Malta. You can wake up to a sunny morning, experience a brief but intense downpour in the afternoon, and then enjoy a beautiful sunset in the evening. It's all part of the Maltese charm, and it's a reminder that you're living on a small island in the middle of the Mediterranean. Be prepared for anything, and always carry an umbrella, just in case.

The Maltese climate is generally considered to be healthy and beneficial. The abundance of sunshine provides vitamin D, which is essential for strong bones and a healthy immune system. The fresh sea air is good for the lungs, and the mild winters are kind to those with joint pain or other ailments. The Mediterranean diet, with its emphasis on fresh produce and olive oil, also contributes to the overall health and well-being of the Maltese people.

However, the heat can be a challenge for some people, especially during the summer months. If you're not used to hot weather, it's important to take precautions to avoid heatstroke and dehydration. Drink plenty of water, avoid strenuous activity during the hottest part of the day, and wear light, loose-fitting clothing. And, of course, take advantage of the siesta to escape the heat and recharge your batteries.

One of the things you'll need to adjust to in Malta is the lack of distinct seasons, especially if you're coming from a country with a more temperate climate. You won't experience the dramatic changes in temperature and foliage that you might be used to. Instead, you'll have a long, hot summer, a mild winter, and two relatively short transitional seasons. It's a different rhythm of life, and it takes some getting used to.

The Maltese landscape is also affected by the climate. The lack of rainfall during the summer months means that the vegetation can become dry and brown. You won't see the lush green fields and forests that you might find in other parts of Europe. Instead, you'll see a landscape of rocky hills, terraced fields, and drought-resistant plants. It's a different kind of beauty, and it's a testament to the resilience of nature.

Despite the challenges of the heat and the occasional storms, the Maltese climate is one of the island's greatest assets. It's a major draw for tourists and expats alike, and it's a key factor in the Maltese way of life. The abundance of sunshine, the warm sea, and the mild winters allow for a year-round outdoor lifestyle, and they contribute to the relaxed and laid-back atmosphere that characterizes Malta.

If you're planning to move to Malta, it's important to be prepared for the climate. Pack light, breathable clothing for the summer months, and bring layers for the winter. Invest in good quality sunscreen, a hat, and sunglasses. And be prepared to adjust your lifestyle to the rhythm of the sun and the sea. It's a different way of life, but it's one that many people find incredibly rewarding.

One of the things you'll need to consider is how the climate will affect your housing choices. If you're renting or buying a property, look for features that will help you cope with the heat, such as air conditioning, good ventilation, and shaded outdoor areas. Thick walls and traditional Maltese features, such as stone floors and high ceilings, can also help to keep the property cool. It's all part of the building design.

In the winter, you might need to use heating, especially in older buildings that are not well-insulated. Electric heaters are common, but they can be expensive to run. Some properties have central heating, but it's not as widespread as in colder climates. It's a good idea to check the heating options when you're looking for a property, and to factor in the potential cost of heating during the winter months.

The Maltese climate can also affect your health and well-being. If you have any pre-existing medical conditions, such as respiratory problems or allergies, it's important to discuss them with your doctor before you move to Malta. The heat, the humidity, and the dust can exacerbate some conditions, and you might need to take extra precautions. It's also a good idea to have a plan in place for dealing with any health issues that might arise.

Despite the challenges, the Maltese climate is generally a positive factor for most expats. It's a chance to enjoy a more outdoor lifestyle, to soak up the vitamin D, and to escape the cold, dark winters of northern Europe. It's a different way of life, and it requires some adjustments, but it's also a rewarding experience that can improve your health, your well-being, and your overall quality of life.

One of the things you'll quickly learn to appreciate in Malta is the importance of shade. Whether it's a strategically placed umbrella on the beach, a shady tree in a park, or a covered terrace on your property, shade is a precious commodity in Malta. It provides a welcome respite from the intense sun, and it can make a significant difference to your comfort level. You'll find yourself seeking out shade whenever possible.

Another thing you'll learn to appreciate is the power of a good breeze. A gentle breeze can make even the hottest day feel bearable, and it's a natural form of air conditioning. You'll find yourself positioning yourself to catch the breeze, whether it's on the beach, on your balcony, or even just standing near an open window. It's a simple pleasure, but it's one that you'll come to cherish.

The Maltese climate is not just about the weather; it's about a way of life. It's about slowing down, taking your time, and enjoying the simple pleasures of life. It's about embracing the siesta, spending time outdoors, and appreciating the beauty of the natural world. It's about adapting to the rhythm of the sun and the sea, and finding a balance between activity and relaxation.

So, prepare for the sun, the heat, the occasional storm, and the ever-present sea breeze. Embrace the Maltese climate, and let it shape your lifestyle, your activities, and your overall experience of living on this beautiful Mediterranean island. It's a climate that will challenge you, surprise you, and ultimately, reward you with a healthier, happier, and more fulfilling way of life. Just don't forget the sunscreen. Seriously, don't.

One thing that can be a bit confusing about the weather in Malta is the difference between the actual temperature and the "feels like" temperature. The "feels like" temperature takes into account factors such as humidity, wind speed, and solar radiation, and it can give a more accurate indication of how hot or cold it actually feels outside. So even if it is hot, it may feel even hotter.

The "feels like" temperature can be significantly higher than the actual temperature during the summer months, especially when the humidity is high. This is because the body cools itself through sweating, and when the humidity is high, the sweat doesn't evaporate as easily, making it feel hotter. So even if the thermometer says 30°C, it might feel like 35°C or even 40°C.

Conversely, the "feels like" temperature can be lower than the actual temperature during the winter months, especially when the wind is strong. This is because the wind increases the rate of heat loss from the body, making it feel colder. So even if the thermometer says 15°C, it might feel like 10°C or even 5°C. It's all a bit of a meteorological mystery.

Another thing to be aware of is that the weather can vary significantly from one part of Malta to another. Due to the island's topography and the influence of the sea, some areas might be sunnier, windier, or rainier than others. For example, the north of the island tends to be windier than the south, and the higher elevations, such as Dingli Cliffs, tend to be cooler and cloudier.

CHAPTER TWENTY-THREE: Taxes: Don't Panic! (But Do Consult an Expert)

Right, let's talk about taxes. The word alone is enough to send shivers down the spine of even the most seasoned expat. But fear not, intrepid adventurer! Maltese taxes, while certainly a reality, aren't the fire-breathing dragon you might imagine. They're more like a slightly grumpy, but ultimately manageable, chihuahua. You need to understand the rules, but with a bit of knowledge and the right advice, you can keep your tax affairs in order without losing your sanity (or your shirt).

Think of the Maltese tax system as a two-tiered cake. The bottom layer is the personal income tax, which applies to your salary, wages, and other income. The top layer is the corporate tax, which applies to the profits of companies. There are other taxes, such as VAT (Value Added Tax) and social security contributions, but these are the two main ones you'll need to be aware of. The system is relatively straightforward, but, as always in Malta, there are quirks and complexities.

First, let's clarify your tax residency. This is crucial, as it determines which taxes you're liable for and how your income is taxed. Generally, you're considered a tax resident in Malta if you spend more than 183 days in Malta in a calendar year. There are other factors that can affect your tax residency, such as your permanent home, your center of vital interests, and your habitual abode. But the 183-day rule is the main one.

If you're a tax resident in Malta, you're generally taxed on your worldwide income. This means that you're liable to pay Maltese tax on any income you earn, regardless of where it comes from. However, Malta has double taxation treaties with many countries, which means that you might not have to pay tax twice on the same income. These treaties can be complex, and it's a good idea to seek professional advice if you have income from multiple sources.

If you're not a tax resident in Malta, you're generally only taxed on income that arises in Malta. This means that if you're working remotely for a foreign company, and you're not a tax resident in Malta, you might not be liable for Maltese income tax. However, there are exceptions to this rule, and it's important to check your specific circumstances with the Maltese tax authorities or a tax advisor.

The personal income tax system in Malta is progressive, which means that the tax rate increases as your income increases. The tax rates range from 0% to 35%, with different tax bands applying to different levels of income. There are also various tax deductions and credits available, which can reduce your tax liability. These include deductions for medical expenses, childcare fees, and contributions to pension schemes. It's important to be aware of it.

The tax year in Malta is the calendar year, from January 1st to December 31st. If you're employed, your employer will deduct tax from your salary each month under the Final Settlement System (FSS). This is similar to the PAYE (Pay As You Earn) system in other countries. Your employer will calculate your tax liability based on your income and any applicable deductions and credits, and they'll pay the tax directly to the Inland Revenue Department (IRD).

At the end of the tax year, your employer will provide you with a statement showing your total income and the amount of tax that has been deducted. You can use this statement to check that the correct amount of tax has been paid. If you think there's been an error, or if you're entitled to any additional deductions or credits, you can file a tax return to claim a refund.

If you're self-employed, you're responsible for calculating and paying your own tax. You'll need to register with the IRD as a self-employed person, and you'll need to file an annual tax return by the deadline, which is usually June 30th of the following year. You'll also need to make provisional tax payments throughout the year, based on your estimated income. It's important to keep accurate records of your income and expenses.

The tax return can be filed online or by mail. It's a relatively straightforward form, but it can be a bit daunting if you're not familiar with the Maltese tax system. You'll need to provide details of your income, any applicable deductions and credits, and any tax that has already been paid. If you're unsure about anything, it's always a good idea to seek professional advice. You do not want to be wrong.

The corporate tax system in Malta is a bit more complex than the personal income tax system. The standard corporate tax rate is 35%, which is relatively high compared to some other European countries. However, Malta operates a full imputation system, which means that shareholders can claim a refund of the tax paid by the company on the profits that are distributed to them as dividends. This can significantly reduce the effective tax rate.

Malta also offers a number of tax incentives for companies, particularly those operating in certain sectors or engaged in international activities. These incentives can include tax credits, reduced tax rates, and exemptions from certain taxes. The rules governing these incentives are complex, and it's important to seek professional advice to ensure that you're complying with all the requirements. It is a good idea to consult an expert.

One of the most attractive tax incentives for companies is the Malta Enterprise scheme, which offers a range of benefits for businesses that invest in Malta and create jobs. These benefits can include tax credits, grants, and soft loans. The scheme is aimed at attracting foreign investment and promoting economic growth in Malta. It's worth exploring if you're planning to start a business in Malta. Talk to a consultant.

Another important aspect of the Maltese tax system is social security contributions. These are mandatory payments that are made by both employees and employers, and they fund the social security system, which provides benefits such as pensions, healthcare, and unemployment benefits. The social security contributions are calculated as a percentage of your income, and they're deducted from your salary each month. They are similar to systems in other countries.

The social security contribution rates vary depending on your income and your employment status. There are different rates for employees, self-employed persons, and non-employed persons. The rates are also subject to a maximum and minimum contribution, which are adjusted annually. It's important to be aware of your social security obligations and to ensure that you're making the correct contributions. It is vital that you are compliant.

If you're an expat working in Malta, you might be eligible for a refund of your social security contributions when you leave Malta permanently. This depends on your nationality, the length of time you've been working in Malta, and the social security agreements that Malta has with your home country. It's a good idea to check with the Maltese social security authorities or a tax advisor to see if you're eligible for a refund.

Value Added Tax (VAT) is another tax that you'll encounter in Malta. VAT is a consumption tax that's applied to most goods and services. The standard VAT rate in Malta is 18%, but there are reduced rates for certain goods and services, such as food, books, and medical services. If you're running a business in Malta, you'll need to register for VAT if your turnover exceeds a certain threshold. This is a complicated subject.

If you're registered for VAT, you'll need to charge VAT on your sales and collect it from your customers. You'll also need to pay VAT on your purchases, but you can usually reclaim this VAT from the tax authorities. You'll need to file regular VAT returns, reporting your sales and purchases, and paying any VAT due or claiming any VAT refund. It's a complex system, and it's important to keep accurate records.

Dealing with taxes in Malta can be a bit daunting, especially if you're not familiar with the local tax system. There are numerous rules, regulations, and deadlines to keep track of, and the penalties for non-compliance can be severe. It's always a good idea to seek professional advice from a tax advisor or an accountant who specializes in Maltese tax matters. They can be really helpful.

A tax advisor can help you understand your tax obligations, ensure that you're complying with all the rules and regulations, and minimize your tax liability. They can also represent you in dealings with the tax authorities and help you resolve any tax disputes. It's an additional expense, but it can save you a lot of time, stress, and potential penalties in the long run. It is often well worth the money.

One of the things that often surprises expats is the relatively informal approach to tax compliance in Malta. While the tax authorities are becoming more stringent, there's still a culture of "creative accounting" and a willingness to bend the rules. This doesn't mean that you should try to evade taxes, but it does mean that you might encounter situations where the rules are not strictly enforced. Be very careful, however.

Another thing that often surprises expats is the importance of personal connections in dealing with the tax authorities. As mentioned earlier, Malta is a small country, and everyone seems to know everyone. This means that personal relationships can often play a role in how things get done. If you know someone who works in the tax department, they might be able to help you navigate the system or speed up a process.

Despite the challenges, the Maltese tax system is generally considered to be fair and transparent. The tax rates are relatively low compared to some other European countries, and there are a number of tax incentives available for individuals and businesses. The system is constantly evolving, and the tax authorities are working to improve compliance and make the system more efficient.

One of the things that's important to remember is that taxes are a contribution to society. They fund public services, such as healthcare, education, and infrastructure. While it's natural to want to minimize your tax liability, it's also important to recognize the role that taxes play in creating a functioning and prosperous society. It's a balance between paying your fair share and ensuring that you're not overpaying.

If you're planning to move to Malta, it's essential to understand the tax implications of your move. You'll need to determine your tax residency, understand your tax obligations, and take steps to ensure that you're complying with all the rules and regulations. It's a complex area, and it's always a good idea to seek professional advice before you make any decisions. It is vital to be compliant.

One of the things you'll need to consider is how your income will be taxed in Malta. If you're employed, your employer will deduct tax from your salary each month under the Final Settlement System (FSS). If you're self-employed, you'll need to register with the IRD and file an annual tax return. If you have income from other sources, such as investments or rental properties, you'll need to declare this income on your tax return.

You'll also need to consider the implications of any double taxation treaties that Malta has with your home country. These treaties can affect how your income is taxed and can prevent you from being taxed twice on the same income. It's important to understand the provisions of the relevant treaty and to ensure that you're claiming any benefits or exemptions that you're entitled to. You should take advice on this.

Another thing you'll need to consider is your social security contributions. If you're working in Malta, you'll need to make social security contributions, which fund the social security system. The contribution rates vary depending on your income and your employment status. You might also be eligible for a refund of your contributions when you leave Malta permanently. It's important to be aware of it.

If you're planning to start a business in Malta, you'll need to understand the corporate tax system and any applicable tax incentives. The standard corporate tax rate is 35%, but there are a number of ways to reduce your effective tax rate. You'll also need to register your company with the Malta Business Registry and comply with all the relevant company laws and regulations. It is not particularly difficult.

Dealing with taxes in Malta is an ongoing process, not a one-time event. You'll need to keep up to date with any changes in the tax laws and regulations, and you'll need to ensure that you're complying with all your obligations on an ongoing basis. It's a good idea to review your tax affairs regularly and to seek professional advice if you have any questions or concerns.

One of the things that can make dealing with taxes in Malta easier is to use online resources and tools. The Inland Revenue Department (IRD) website provides a wealth of information on the Maltese tax system, including tax guides, forms, and online services. You can also use online tax calculators to estimate your tax liability and to check that you're paying the correct amount of tax.

Another helpful resource is the Malta Institute of Taxation, which is a professional body for tax advisors and accountants in Malta. The institute provides training and resources for its members, and it also publishes information on tax matters for the general public. You can find a list of registered tax advisors on the institute's website.

Ultimately, dealing with taxes in Malta is about understanding the rules, seeking professional advice when needed, and being organized and proactive. It's not the most exciting aspect of expat life, but it's an essential one. By taking the time to understand your tax obligations and to manage your tax affairs effectively, you can avoid unnecessary stress and penalties, and you can focus on enjoying your new life in Malta.

CHAPTER TWENTY-FOUR: Leaving Malta: The Reverse Culture Shock (and Missing the *Pastizzi*)

So, the time has come. You're leaving Malta. Maybe you've achieved your goals, maybe you're ready for a new adventure, or maybe you've just had enough of roundabouts and *pastizzi* (unlikely, but possible). Whatever the reason, you're packing your bags, saying your goodbyes, and preparing to re-enter the "real world." But be warned, departing from this quirky little island is not as simple as boarding a plane and waving goodbye. It involves a whole new set of challenges.

Think of leaving Malta as the final boss battle in your expat video game. You've leveled up your patience, conquered the bureaucracy, and mastered the art of driving on the left (mostly). Now, you face the ultimate test: reverse culture shock. It's the disorienting feeling of returning to your home country and realizing that everything is both familiar and strangely different. It's like stepping into a parallel universe where people drive on the "wrong" side of the road.

First, there's the practical side of leaving. You'll need to terminate your rental agreement, close your bank accounts, cancel your utilities, and notify the relevant authorities of your departure. It's essentially the reverse of everything you did when you arrived, but with the added emotional baggage of saying goodbye to a place that, despite its quirks, has become your home. It's a bittersweet process, and it's important to allow yourself time to grieve the loss.

Terminating your rental agreement should be relatively straightforward, provided you've followed the terms of your lease. Give your landlord the required notice, usually one or two months, and arrange a final inspection of the property. Make sure the property is clean and in good condition, and take photos as evidence, just in case there are any disputes about the deposit. It's always better to be prepared and to protect yourself from potential problems.

Closing your bank accounts can be a bit more complicated, especially if you have any outstanding loans or credit cards. You'll need to visit your bank in person, provide identification, and sign some forms. It's a good idea to withdraw any remaining funds in cash, as transferring money internationally can involve fees and delays. And make sure you get a written confirmation that your accounts have been closed, just in case.

Canceling your utilities, such as electricity, water, and internet, involves contacting the respective providers and giving them your final meter readings. You'll need to provide your account details and your forwarding address for the final bills. It's a good idea to do this a few weeks before you leave, to avoid any unexpected charges or delays. And make sure you keep copies of all the correspondence, just in case.

You'll also need to notify Identity Malta of your departure, especially if you have a residence permit. This is important to avoid any complications with your immigration status and to ensure that you're not liable for any taxes or other obligations after you leave. You can usually do this by visiting the Expatriates Unit at Identity Malta and filling out a form. It's a relatively straightforward process, but it's an essential step.

If you have children in school, you'll need to inform the school of your departure and arrange for their school records to be transferred to their new school. It's a good idea to do this well in advance, as it can take time to process the paperwork. You might also need to obtain certified copies of your children's birth certificates and other documents, depending on the requirements of their new school.

If you own a car in Malta, you'll need to either sell it or export it. Selling a car in Malta can be a bit of a hassle, as the market is relatively small, and you might not get the price you're hoping for. You can advertise your car online or through local newspapers, or you can try selling it to a car dealer. Exporting a car involves more paperwork and expense.

You'll need to deregister the car with Transport Malta, obtain an export certificate, and arrange for the car to be shipped to your destination country. You'll also need to comply with the import regulations of your destination country, which can vary significantly. It's a complex process, and it's often easier to sell the car in Malta, unless it has sentimental value or it's a particularly valuable model. Consider the complications first.

If you have pets, you'll need to arrange for their transport back to your home country or to your next destination. As discussed in Chapter Seventeen, this involves obtaining the necessary health certificates, vaccinations, and pet passports. You'll also need to book flights for your pets and ensure that they're comfortable and safe during the journey. It's a stressful process, but it's essential for the well-being of your furry friends.

Once you've dealt with the practicalities, you'll need to start packing your belongings. This can be a daunting task, especially if you've accumulated a lot of stuff during your time in Malta. You'll need to decide what to take with you, what to sell or donate, and what to throw away. It's a good opportunity to declutter and to get rid of anything you don't need or use.

If you're shipping your belongings, you'll need to choose a reputable shipping company and arrange for your belongings to be packed and transported. The cost of shipping can vary significantly depending on the volume of your belongings, the destination, and the shipping method. It's a good idea to get quotes from several different companies and to compare their services and prices. And consider insuring your stuff, also.

If you're taking your belongings with you on the plane, you'll need to comply with the airline's baggage restrictions. Each airline has its own rules regarding the size, weight, and number of bags you can check in and carry on. It's important to check these rules carefully before you pack, to avoid any unexpected fees or delays at the airport. And be prepared to pay extra for excess baggage.

Leaving Malta is not just about logistics; it's also about saying goodbye. It's about saying goodbye to the friends you've made, the places you've come to love, and the experiences you've shared. It's about acknowledging that a chapter of your life is coming to an end, and that you're moving on to something new. It's a bittersweet experience, and it's important to allow yourself time to process your emotions.

One of the things that many expats miss most about Malta is the sense of community. The small size of the island and the close-knit nature of Maltese society create a strong sense of belonging. You'll miss the friendly faces, the casual conversations, and the feeling of being part of something bigger than yourself. It's a unique aspect of Maltese life, and it's something that's hard to replicate in other places.

Another thing you'll likely miss is the Maltese lifestyle. The relaxed pace of life, the emphasis on family and friends, the abundance of sunshine, and the access to the sea. You'll miss the siestas, the *festas*, and the long, leisurely meals. You'll miss the simple pleasures of life that Malta offers in abundance. It's a lifestyle that's hard to leave behind. And it's one you'll crave.

And, of course, you'll miss the *pastizzi*. Those flaky, cheesy, delicious pastries that have become a staple of your Maltese diet. You'll miss the smell of them baking in the *pastizzerias*, the taste of them fresh from the oven, and the comfort they provide on a cold day or a late night. You'll try to find them in your home country, but they'll never be quite the same.

But leaving Malta is not just about missing things; it's also about looking forward to the future. It's about embracing new opportunities, new challenges, and new experiences. It's about taking the lessons you've learned in Malta and applying them to your next adventure. It's about growing, evolving, and becoming a more resilient and adaptable person. It's a journey, not a destination.

When you return to your home country, you'll likely experience reverse culture shock. Things that once seemed normal will now seem strange. You might find yourself driving on the wrong side of the road, instinctively reaching for your Maltese phone number, or craving a *pastizz* at 3 am. You might find yourself missing the chaos of Maltese traffic, the warmth of the Maltese people, or the simplicity of Maltese life.

Reverse culture shock can be just as disorienting as the initial culture shock you experienced when you arrived in Malta. It's a sign that you've changed, that you've grown, and that you've been affected by your time in Malta. It's a normal part of the expat experience, and it's important to allow yourself time to adjust. Be patient with yourself, be open to new experiences, and don't be afraid to talk about your feelings.

One of the best ways to cope with reverse culture shock is to stay connected with your Malta friends. Thanks to social media and the internet, it's easier than ever to keep in touch with people across the globe. You can share your experiences, reminisce about your time in Malta, and support each other through the transition. It's a valuable lifeline, and it can help you feel less alone.

Another way to cope with reverse culture shock is to find ways to incorporate elements of the Maltese lifestyle into your new life. Maybe you can learn to cook Maltese dishes, find a local Mediterranean restaurant, or join a Maltese cultural group. Maybe you can start taking siestas, spending more time outdoors, or simply slowing down and appreciating the simple pleasures of life. It's about finding a balance.

Leaving Malta is a significant life event, and it's important to approach it with the same care and attention that you gave to your arrival. It's a time for reflection, for closure, and for new beginnings. It's a time to say goodbye to one chapter of your life and to embrace the next. It's a time to celebrate your achievements, to learn from your mistakes, and to look forward to the future with hope and optimism.

One thing that is important to remember is to keep your Maltese bank account open, at least for a while. This will make it easier to receive any final payments, such as refunds or tax rebates. And it will make it easier to pay any outstanding bills. You can always close it later, once everything has been finalized. But keeping it open initially will save you from headaches.

Another consideration is informing utility companies, and other companies, of your new address. This is so that they can send any final bills or statements to you. And so that they know where to contact you, if necessary. This can be done online, in most cases. But it is important to do it, to avoid any complications. And keep records of having done so, for future reference.

Leaving Malta can be a significant life event. But it need not be stressful, if you are properly prepared. It is a case of planning, and of making arrangements in advance. And of being organized. If you do these things, your departure from Malta can be smooth and trouble-free. And you can then look forward to the next chapter in your life, whatever that may be.

And you will take with you memories of Malta. Memories of the sun, the sea, the *pastizzi*, and the people. Memories of the good times, and the challenging times. Memories that will stay with you for the rest of your life. And who knows, you may even return to Malta one day. Many expats do. Because Malta has a way of getting under your skin.

So be prepared for leaving. It may seem a long way off when you arrive. But the time will come. And it will come sooner than you think. So make plans for it. Be organized. And do not leave everything to the last minute. If you follow this advice, you will have a much smoother experience when it is time to move on. And to wherever you are going next.

So that is it. Leaving Malta. It is the end of one chapter, and the start of another. It can be a sad time. But it can also be an exciting time. A time of new beginnings. And a time to look forward to the future. So embrace it. And make the most of it. And take with you the memories of your time in Malta.

CHAPTER TWENTY-FIVE: The Final Verdict: Is Malta *Really* Worth It? (Spoiler Alert: Maybe)

Right, you've made it. You've survived the visa gauntlet, the housing hunt, the banking bewilderment, the driving madness, and the bureaucratic labyrinth. You've learned to love (or at least tolerate) *pastizzi*, mastered the art of the siesta, and maybe even picked up a few Maltese phrases. You've experienced the sun, the sea, the chaos, and the charm of this quirky little island nation. Now, the ultimate question: was it worth it?

Well, *mela*, that depends. There's no simple yes or no answer. Malta, like any country, has its pros and cons, its ups and downs, its moments of pure bliss and its moments of utter frustration. It's a place that will challenge you, surprise you, and probably change you in ways you never expected. Whether it's "worth it" is a deeply personal question, and the answer will depend on your individual circumstances, your priorities, and your tolerance for roundabouts.

Let's recap the good stuff. Malta offers a unique blend of Mediterranean lifestyle, rich history, and a vibrant expat community. The climate is fantastic, with over 300 days of sunshine per year, and the sea is crystal clear and inviting. The cost of living, while not as cheap as some might expect, is still relatively affordable compared to many other European countries. And the tax system can be quite favorable, especially for certain types of income.

The Maltese people are generally warm and welcoming, and the expat community is diverse and supportive. There are plenty of opportunities to socialize, make friends, and explore the island's many attractions. The food is delicious, the culture is fascinating, and the pace of life is generally relaxed. It's a place where you can enjoy a good work-life balance, spend plenty of time outdoors, and embrace a more laid-back approach to life.

But, and there's always a but, Malta is not paradise. It's a small, densely populated island, with limited space and resources. The infrastructure can be creaky, the bureaucracy can be maddening, and the driving can be terrifying. The summers are hot and humid, the winters can be surprisingly chilly, and the power cuts and water shortages can be frustrating. It's a place that requires patience, adaptability, and a good sense of humor.

One of the biggest challenges for many expats is the size of Malta. It's *small*. Really small. You can drive across the entire country in less than an hour, and you'll quickly become familiar with every nook and cranny of the island. This can be both a blessing and a curse. On the one hand, it's easy to get around, and you're never far from the sea or the countryside. On the other, you can feel a bit claustrophobic.

Another challenge is the Maltese bureaucracy, as we've discussed *ad nauseam*. Dealing with officialdom in Malta can be a frustrating and time-consuming experience. The rules are often unclear, the processes are unnecessarily complicated, and the outcome is frequently unpredictable. You'll need patience, persistence, and a willingness to navigate a system that seems designed to test your sanity. It's a national sport, after all. Just not a fun one, particularly.

The driving in Malta, as we've also covered extensively, is another major challenge. The narrow streets, the chaotic traffic, and the, um, *unique* driving style of the Maltese can be intimidating for newcomers. You'll need to be assertive, but not aggressive, and you'll need to anticipate the unpredictable behavior of other drivers. It's a constant learning experience, and it's not for the faint of heart. But you knew that.

The cost of living in Malta, while generally lower than in some other European countries, is not as cheap as some people might expect. Rent, in particular, can be quite high, especially in the popular areas. And imported goods are often more expensive than in other countries, due to the cost of shipping everything to a small island. You'll need to budget carefully and be prepared to adjust your spending habits.

Another challenge for some expats is the language barrier. While English is widely spoken, Maltese is the national language, and it's used in many aspects of daily life. Learning some Maltese can be helpful, but it's not essential for survival. However, it can limit your ability to fully integrate into Maltese society and to understand the nuances of the local culture. It's a trade-off between convenience and cultural immersion.

Despite the challenges, many expats find that Malta is a wonderful place to live. It offers a unique combination of factors that are hard to find elsewhere: a Mediterranean climate, a rich history, a vibrant culture, a relaxed pace of life, and a relatively low cost of living. It's a place where you can enjoy a good quality of life, make new friends, and pursue your passions. But all good things come at a price.

One of the things that often surprises expats is how quickly they adapt to the Maltese way of life. The initial culture shock fades, the frustrations become less intense, and the quirks become endearing. You start to appreciate the slower pace of life, the importance of family and community, and the simple pleasures of a sunny day and a good meal. You learn to navigate the bureaucracy, the traffic, and the occasional power cut.

You also start to develop a deeper understanding of Maltese culture. You learn about the history, the traditions, and the values of the Maltese people. You appreciate the warmth and hospitality, the direct communication style, and the passionate debates about politics and football. You learn to laugh at the chaos, to embrace the unexpected, and to find the humor in even the most frustrating situations.

And you start to feel like you belong. You make friends, you build a support network, and you create a new home for yourself. You discover your favorite *pastizzeria*, your favorite beach, and your favorite walking route. You find your place in the Maltese community, and you start to feel like you're part of something bigger than yourself. It's a gradual process, but it's a rewarding one.

So, is Malta *really* worth it? The answer, ultimately, is up to you. It depends on what you're looking for in a new home, what your priorities are, and what your tolerance is for the inevitable challenges that come with living in a foreign country. If you're looking for a perfectly organized, predictable, and utterly boring existence, then Malta is probably not for you. But few expats are.

If, on the other hand, you're looking for an adventure, a challenge, and a chance to experience a different way of life, then Malta might just be the perfect place for you. It's a place that will test your patience, push your boundaries, and force you to adapt to new situations. But it's also a place that will reward you with sunshine, sea, delicious food, and a vibrant community.

It's a place where you can reinvent yourself, pursue your passions, and create a life that's both fulfilling and meaningful. It's a place where you can learn new things, meet new people, and discover a new side of yourself. It's a place that will stay with you long after you've left, shaping your perspectives and enriching your life in countless ways. It is somewhere you will never forget.

But it's also a place that requires commitment, effort, and a willingness to embrace the unexpected. It's not a holiday destination; it's a place to live, work, and build a life. You'll encounter challenges, frustrations, and moments of doubt. But you'll also experience moments of joy, connection, and pure, unadulterated happiness. It's a rollercoaster ride, and it's up to you to decide if you're willing to take the plunge.

So, before you make the leap, do your research, weigh the pros and cons, and be honest with yourself about what you're looking for. Talk to other expats, visit Malta if you can, and get a feel for the place. Don't rely solely on glossy brochures or romanticized blog posts. Get the real picture, the unvarnished truth, and make an informed decision.

And if you do decide to move to Malta, be prepared for an adventure. Be prepared for the chaos, the bureaucracy, the driving madness, and the occasional power cut. But also be prepared for the sunshine, the sea, the delicious food, the warm hospitality, and the vibrant community. Be prepared to be challenged, surprised, and ultimately, transformed by this quirky little island nation.

Because, despite its flaws, Malta has a way of getting under your skin. It's a place that captivates you, challenges you, and ultimately, makes you feel alive. It's a place that you might love, you might hate, but you'll definitely never forget. And, who knows, you might just find that it's the best decision you ever made. Or, at the very least, a *very* interesting one.

So that's it. The final verdict. Is Malta worth it? Maybe. Probably. It depends. It's up to you. But if you're willing to take the leap, to embrace the chaos, and to open yourself up to the possibilities, you might just find that this tiny rock in the Mediterranean is exactly the place you've been looking for. Or, you might end up running for the hills, screaming about roundabouts and *pastizzi*. Either way, it's going to be an adventure.

And just remember all the things we've covered in this book. They will be useful. They will help you to adjust to Maltese life. And they will help you to decide whether Malta is the place for you. Or not. But either way, you will have made an informed decision. And that is the important thing. You will have moved here with your eyes open.

And even if you don't stay forever, you will have had an experience. An experience that will change you. An experience that you will never forget. And an experience that will give you a new perspective on life. And that, in itself, is worth something. It may be worth a lot. It may be worth more than you realize.

So go on, take the plunge. Or don't. It's your decision. But if you do, be prepared for a wild ride. A ride that will take you to places you never expected. A ride that will challenge you in ways you never imagined. And a ride that will ultimately leave you with a